DECISIONS
MATTER

NASPA
Student Affairs Administrators
in Higher Education

Using a Decision-Making Framework with Contemporary Student Affairs Case Studies

DECISIONS MATTER

Foreword by Susan R. Komives and Mike Segawa

Annemarie Vaccaro, Brian McCoy, Delight Champagne, and Michael Siegel

NASPA

Student Affairs Administrators
in Higher Education

Decisions Matter: Using a Decision-Making Framework with Contemporary Student Affairs Case Studies

Published by
NASPA–Student Affairs Administrators in Higher Education
111 K Street, NE
10th Floor
Washington, DC 20002
www.naspa.org

Additional copies may be purchased by contacting the NASPA publications department at 301-638-1749 or visiting http://bookstore.naspa.org.

NASPA does not discriminate on the basis of race, color, national origin, religion, sex, age, gender identity, gender expression, affectional or sexual orientation, or disability in any of its policies, programs, and services.

Library of Congress Cataloging-in-Publication Data

Vaccaro, Annemarie, author.
  Decisions matter : using a decision-making framework with contemporary student affairs case studies / Annemarie Vaccaro, Brian McCoy, Delight Champagne, and Michael Siegel.
     pages cm
  Includes bibliographical references and index.
  ISBN 978-0-931654-85-5
  1. Student affairs services--United States--Decision making. 2. Student affairs services--United States--Case studies. I. Title.
  LB2342.92.V33 2013
  378.1'970973--dc23
                    2012051403

Printed and bound in the United States of America

FIRST EDITION

Contents

Susan R. Komives and Mike Segawa

Acknowledgments

WE ARE DEEPLY grateful to a number of people who provided us with guidance, insight, and support during our work on *Decisions Matter*. We first wish to express our sincere gratitude to Jean G. Beaupré, visiting assistant professor of marketing and business communication at Nichols College, who provided us with the pictorial representation of the decision-making framework (DMF). She was able to take our thoughts, words, and concepts and create an icon that is not only easy to follow but also aesthetically pleasing.

Many friends, colleagues, and students at our home institutions as well as in NASPA Region I offered us their expertise, enthusiasm, and encouragement. Their personal and professional support was invaluable to the creation of *Decisions Matter*. In particular, we wish to thank the members of the Region I Faculty Summit, whose discussion on the need for reflective and practical learning experiences for graduate students and new professionals was the genesis of this book. We also wish to thank our graduate students at Springfield College, Suffolk University, and the University of Rhode Island, as well as members of Region I who attended our conference presentation of the DMF, for their honest and thoughtful critiques. Their comments and feedback helped us refine the DMF into a workable and easily applicable decision-making process for student affairs professionals.

A special acknowledgment goes to the many people who helped us with technical aspects of the project or graciously gave us a place to meet and work. We thank Joe Ginese, first-year and new student experience specialist at the Borough of Manhattan Community College, for his assistance in the development of our Call for Cases database and website, and

David Earnhardt, career counselor at the University of Massachusetts Boston, for producing our advertising materials. Our warmest appreciation goes to Justin Dolan, conference and events manager at Nichols College; Kristin King Salemi, director of the student union at Rhode Island College; and Jacqueline Peterson, vice president of student affairs and dean of students at the College of the Holy Cross, for providing us with meeting space and amazing hospitality.

We would also like to thank Shawn DeVeau, interim director of enrollment services and university registrar, University of Texas, Medical Branch; Barbara Fienman, interim administrator and consultant; Matthew Haggard, instructional services/reference librarian at Nichols College; and Liz Horgan, director of career services at Nichols College, for helping us locate supplementary resources to make the case analyses richer and more meaningful. Deep thanks also go to Andrew Gresenz, graduate resident director and higher education graduate student, Suffolk University (formerly undergraduate intern in the Student Affairs Office at Nichols College), for the many hours he spent organizing, categorizing, and searching for material for this book. We could not have completed this project so thoroughly without him.

A number of people provided us with case suggestions and meaningful examples to consider. Thanks to Daniel Adams, Clemson University; Cara Appel-Silbaugh, Georgia Institute of Technology; Mark Bauman, Bloomsburg University; Jennifer Lease Butts, University of Connecticut; Joelle Davis Carter, Western Kentucky University; Cathy Cocks, University of Connecticut; Rod Crafts, Olin College; Kerry W. Foxx, Syracuse University; Maria Elisa Grandone, Loyola Marymount University; Steven Harowitz, University of South Carolina; Sandrine Heeren, Virginia Commonwealth University; Ciarra Joyner, University of Tampa; Mitchell A. Levy, LaGuardia Community College; Wade Livingston, Clemson University;

Michael Mann, Illinois State University; Phyllis McCluskey-Titus, Illinois State University; Daryl Minus, Craven Community College; Bernard A. Polnariev, LaGuardia Community College; Paul Porter III, University of Rhode Island; S. Bryan Rush, Erskine College; Amelia Scott, University of Rhode Island; Jennifer Smith, University of South Carolina; and Kristen Whitney, University of Tampa.

We would be remiss if we did not also thank the NASPA staff for their guidance, editorial expertise, and stewardship of the process. Melissa Dahne was particularly instrumental from start to finish in helping us shape and refine the work. Thank you also to the staff, faculty, and students at our home institutions—Nichols College, Springfield College, Suffolk University, and the University of Rhode Island—who supported us in this endeavor. We also sincerely thank Susan R. Komives, professor emerita at the University of Maryland College Park, and Mike Segawa, vice president for student affairs and dean of students at the University of Puget Sound, who graciously accepted our invitation to write a foreword. It is an extraordinary honor to have their involvement in our work.

Finally, we offer our deepest appreciation to our families—Sarah Couch; Donna and Richard Vaccaro; Monique, Andrew, and Benjamin McCoy; Lyle Champagne; Vae and Jim Mecca; Jack and Meghan Champagne; and Meredith, Ben, Natalie, and Allyson Siegel—for their love, understanding, and patience as we worked on this book. Their emotional support and encouragement helped make the book a reality.

The Authors

DELIGHT CHAMPAGNE is a professor of psychology and director of the Student Personnel Administration in Higher Education Program at Springfield College. She comes from a professional background in adult education and career counseling. She holds a PhD in counseling psychology (with specialized areas in adult development and learning, and career development); an MA in guidance, counseling, and personnel from the University of Connecticut; and a BA in psychology from Boston University.

Champagne's research and professional interests have focused on career and adult transitions, young adult development related to sports, and current professional issues in student affairs. Her publications include authored and co-authored chapters in a number of books, including *Toward Administrative Reawakening: Creating and Maintaining Safe College Campuses* (Stylus 2007) and *Athlete's Guide to Career Planning: Keys to Success from the Playing Field to Professional Life* (Human Kinetics 1998); as well as articles in the *Journal of Student Affairs Research and Practice, Academic Athletic Journal, Journal of College Student Development, Journal of Counseling and Development*, and *Adult Education Quarterly*.

Champagne has been active in numerous professional organizations. As a member of NASPA–Student Affairs Administrators in Higher Education, she served on the editorial board of the *Journal of Student Affairs Research and Practice* and was a judge in the National Case Study Competition. In NASPA Region I, she has served as faculty liaison, conference planning committee member, and advisory board member.

BRIAN MCCOY is vice president for student affairs and dean of student services at Nichols College, as well as an adjunct psychology professor at Assumption and Nichols Colleges. His former student affairs positions were in the residence life departments at Wentworth Institute of Technology and Assumption College. He also served as the department manager for the Division of Family Practice at the Fallon Clinic. He holds an EdD in educational policy, research, and administration from the University of Massachusetts Amherst; an MA in counseling psychology from Assumption College, and a BA in psychology from Anna Maria College.

McCoy's publications include the chapter "The Final Six Weeks" in *Ready for the Real World* (Wadsworth 1994), as well as *Fallon 101—A Longitudinal Orientation*, which appeared in the *HMO Journal*. He served as a reviewer for *Taking Sides: Clashing Views in Human Sexuality* (McGraw-Hill 2011) and *The Developing Person: Through the Life Span* (Worth Publishers 2008).

As an active member of NASPA since 1985, he has served in a variety of leadership positions, including Region I conference chair, Region I vice president, Featured Speakers chair for the 2009 NASPA Annual Conference, chair of the 2013 NASPA Annual Conference, and a member of the Task Force on the Future of Student Affairs.

MICHAEL SIEGEL is an associate professor and director of

the Administration of Higher Education Program at Suffolk University in Boston. He is a former research fellow at the Policy Center on the First Year of College, where he was responsible for a wide range of national projects and research initiatives aimed at improving the first college year. He served previously as a project manager for the College Student Experiences Questionnaire at Indiana University. He received his PhD from Indiana University in higher education administration with a minor in anthropology.

Siegel has written several publications and made numerous conference presentations, both in the United States and abroad, on the first college year, college and university culture, and leadership in the college presidency. He co-authored *First-Generation College Students: Understanding and Improving the Experience from Recruitment to Commencement* (Jossey-Bass 2012). His research has been featured in *About Campus*, *Journal of College Orientation and Transition*, and *Journal of Academic Administration in Higher Education.*

Siegel has long been an active member of NASPA and served from 2007 through 2011 on the NASPA Region I advisory board as faculty liaison. He received the 2006 John Brennan Award for Outstanding Instruction from the Suffolk University College of Arts and Sciences.

ANNEMARIE VACCARO is a faculty member in the Department of Human Development and Family Studies, College Student Personnel Program, at the University of Rhode Island. Before joining the faculty, she spent much of her student affairs career working in residence life and in living and learning communities. She holds a PhD in higher education administration and an MA in sociology from the University of Denver. She also has an MA in student affairs from Indiana University of Pennsylvania and a BA from Castleton State College.

Vaccaro's service, teaching, and research interests focus on social justice issues in higher education. She co-authored *Safe Spaces: Making Schools and Communities Welcoming to LGBT Youth* (Praeger 2012). Her research can be found in publications such as the *Journal of Student Affairs Research and Practice*, *NASPA Journal About Women in Higher Education*, *Journal of LGBT Youth*, *Journal of GLBT Family Studies*, *Equity and Excellence in Education*, and *Journal of Gay and Lesbian Mental Health.*

Throughout her career, Vaccaro has been an active member of NASPA. She is currently chair of the Melvene D. Hardee Dissertation of the Year Award committee and is Region I faculty liaison. Previously, she was a coordinator of research in NASPA Region IV-West.

Case Study Contributors

WE WISH TO acknowledge and thank the contributions of the following people whose case submissions appear in *Decisions Matter*. Their contemporary cases are central to this book and offer readers a unique perspective on the challenges faced by student affairs professionals.

Chris Arbeene, University of San Diego

Christine Austin, Arkansas Tech University

O. Gilbert Brown, Missouri State University

Denise Carl, University of Idaho

Amy Carmack, University of Kansas Medical Center

Candace Dennig, Johnson and Wales University

Sandra Estanek, Canisius College

Seth Matthew Fishman, University of North Texas

Chris Giroir, Arkansas Tech University

April Heiselt, Mississippi State University

Khalia Ii, University of Southern California

Daniella Knelman, University of San Diego

Amanda Kraus, University of Arizona

Kim Nehls, University of Nevada, Las Vegas

Isaac Spivey, Springfield College

Tim Wilson, University of San Diego

Arturo Vazquez, Seattle University

Foreword

Susan R. Komives and Mike Segawa

I BEGAN MY career in 1969, during the student protest era. I remember the week in 1971 when a bomb went off in a restroom in the U.S. Capitol. The next day at 11 p.m., my campus received a bomb threat. I was 23 years old and a new professional, but as an area coordinator it was my responsibility to make a decision on whether we would evacuate any residence hall in my complex in the face of such a threat.

I decided this was a very good night to evacuate. The next night, the same thing happened at the same time, and we again evacuated. On the third night, although students anticipated another evacuation (one woman even brought her rocking chair outside ahead of time), my team decided something else was going on and, instead, we did not evacuate. We finally traced the calls to the room of a student in desperate need of attention. The situation changed from a crisis in which I needed to make an immediate decision to a more complex circumstance that required various resources. This was just one of many decisions, large and small, I had to make during my 43 years in the student affairs field—18 as a practitioner and 25 as a graduate faculty member.

The case studies in this book reflect real situations that student affairs professionals have encountered in their daily work. Even if in the course of your own career you never have to deal with many of the types of issues described in this book, you might have a colleague call you for advice on how to handle a scenario on his or her campus. This book assists professionals with anticipating complex scenarios, provides a useful model to approach those challenging situations, and identifies the competencies and philosophies needed to address them. These cases are complicated further in the context of technology, particularly social media. When information is shared so quickly and readily, there is often no time to ponder solutions. Thinking through each case will help you prepare to make critical decisions.

We are fortunate in student affairs to be guided by several transcendent principles that shape professional action. College student personnel graduate programs have courses to introduce new professionals to these principles, such as the "Professional Orientation" course I facilitated at the University of Maryland. Indeed, new professionals need an orientation to the ethics, values, principles, historical perspective, theoretical frames, and related skills and competencies to address today's challenging situations. New professionals should ask their supervisors to put "guiding principles" as a topic on the staff meeting agenda, so teams can identify and commit to beliefs that will guide decision making.

Today's student affairs professional no longer has mere problems to solve. Today's professional is faced with paradoxes and dilemmas. The issues involved can be self-contradictory or the choices are equally right (or wrong) and pose new issues when a decision is made. Applying the decision-making framework (DMF) in this book will help professionals examine the context and complexity of situations and lead to informed decisions. The DMF model (identify, scan, implement, and assess) is a useful heuristic for all professionals.

As I reflect on my years in the student affairs field, there are some lessons learned that served me well, and I offer them for your consideration. Each could be expanded substantially, and I hope they are useful even in their brevity. Most of them are developed further in this book.

- **Principles and beliefs should guide actions.** Considerations of safety and harm must always come first and necessitate quick action. Beyond that, the complexities of issues require us to be guided by professional beliefs. We believe students have rights; we believe each student has dignity and worth; we believe in free speech even if we do not agree with the content; and so on. Learn our professional beliefs and ethical standards, shape those for your office or functional area, and have clear agreement on them among your colleagues. We also believe in turning everything into a teachable moment, a corollary of our core principles. It is useful to adopt former U.S. Secretary John Gardner's perspective: "What we have before us are some breathtaking opportunities disguised as insoluble problems" (PBS, n.d., para. 1). Issues like hate crimes are difficult to handle but can mobilize the campus to affirm values, have transparent learning discussions, and even create new policies and procedures.

- **Both process and outcome matter.** As advanced in this book, I agree wholeheartedly that *how* a decision is made is as central as *what* is decided. Were appropriate individuals or groups consulted, and were their perspectives heard? Concurrently, understand the roles of acceptance and quality in a decision. Different processes are required when both are of high importance, when one is more important than the other, or when neither matter a great deal.

- **Leaders are meaning makers.** How an issue or situation is framed makes a huge difference in how it is perceived by stakeholders. For example, protesters may be portrayed either as "disruptive trouble makers trying to shut down the university" or "passionate leaders exercising free speech and trying to shape a public agenda."

- **Will your actions pass the *Washington Post* sniff test?** My wise friend and colleague Nance Lucas encourages all of us to pause and imagine your process or decisions on the front page of the *Washington Post's* Metro section. Would you be proud of what you did and how you came to that decision? If it feels wrong, it probably is. It may mean learning to point out ethical issues or consequences to supervisors who may have been hasty in their initial judgments. Always seek to do the right thing.

- **Almost every issue calls for multiple partial solutions.** No one approach will likely solve any problem. Think of all the multiple interventions and first steps that can be initiated. Have a system of solutions for the complex dimensions of the issue. Consider almost every non-crisis decision to be formative not summative. Evaluate new programs, procedures, and policies after they have been in place for a period of time. Invite wide input, particularly from those who may have been originally skeptical about the decision, and revise as needed. Context can change quickly; formative reviews can keep a system nimble and responsive.

- **You are never alone.** You will make many decisions each day and have the authority and responsibility to do so. As the authors note in this book, when a decision feels too big to handle on your own, remember you are not alone. Good supervisors will help you think through options quickly, take on the situation if it is beyond the scope of your position, or mobilize parts of the solution while you handle the direct student contact. There is no way, for example, that you should be the one to call a parent to tell them their child is dead. Your institution should have crisis protocols in situations like the death of a student that guide you in the multiple actions to be taken.

Your institution is lucky to have you. As a frontline professional in direct contact with so many students, you have the pulse of the student body. Use your credibility with students to prevent difficult situations, deal with crises, and support students as they manage problems in their own lives. Ensure that all your professional decisions are grounded in the ethics, values, principles, historical perspective, theoretical frames, and related skills and competencies of our field. This book will help you practice these critical decision-making capacities.

Susan R. Komives
Professor Emerita
University of Maryland

TO STATE THE obvious, we in student affairs deal with challenging and consequential situations. As I read the case studies included in this important book, I was reminded of this daily reality in an almost visceral sense. Our decisions matter because they impact the institutions we have the privilege of serving as well as the lives of our students, colleagues, families, and external stakeholders. But this observation is not meant to create anxiety; rather, it is meant to reinforce why a book like *Decisions Matter* is invaluable and long overdue.

Almost a decade ago, Susan Jones and I (2004) wrote in *Job One: Experiences of New Professionals in Student Affairs* of the need for "graduate preparation programs and student affairs professionals to join together in substantive and meaningful ways to develop curriculum and professional development experiences that complement one another and integrate with the core values and contemporary issues of the profession. The distance between graduate preparation programs and professional work, or from theory to practice, should be a short one" (p. 75). In the years after that book's release, I believed that student affairs still lacked a publication that directly addressed this theory-to-practice gap. It is gratifying to see *Decisions Matter* finally tackle this need and do so in such a highly effective manner.

The strength of *Decisions Matter* lies in its integration of research and practice; its use of the seminal work *Professional Competency Areas for Student Affairs Practitioners* (ACPA & NASPA, 2010); its development of a profession-specific decision-making framework; and its inclusion of case studies that are highly relevant to today's profession. Grounding the book in this manner has resulted in a resource that is helpful today and will continue to be valuable for years to come. It is a book whose pages should become dog-eared and tattered from use by faculty, supervisors, and newer colleagues.

Employing this book in the professional development of our newest practitioners is only a start. As the authors note, continuous assessment and constant evolution is an important part of refining our profession and consistently equipping ourselves to be effective educators and administrators. This notion of lifelong learning has always been a key value of our profession, and *Decisions Matter* provides us with a unique resource when it comes to well-grounded and persistent professional development. The theories, decision-making framework, and case studies make this book a professional development tool that will be useful from the first days on the job to the years beyond.

Our work over the years has increased in the demands placed upon us, the complexities of the circumstances confronting us on a regular basis, and the possible consequences to our students, our institutions, and ourselves. Those entering our profession today are faced with a more complicated work environment than the one I entered 30 years ago. This is a daunting reality. The good news, though, is that the preparation of today's professional is immensely stronger than what previous generations were afforded. That is the nature of evolution and the benefit of the ever-increasing sophistication of our student affairs work. *Decisions Matter* significantly adds to our growth as a profession and is an important piece of our continuing effort to better serve our students and institutions. It should become an integral part of any professional's ongoing development plan.

Mike Segawa
Vice President of Student Affairs and Dean of Students
University of Puget Sound

References

American College Personnel Association (ACPA) and National Association of Student Personnel Administrators (NASPA). (2010). *Professional competency areas for student affairs practitioners*. Retrieved from http://www.naspa.org/programs/prodev/Professional_Competencies.pdf

Jones, S. R., & Segawa, M. (2004). Crossing the bridge from graduate school to job one. In P. M. Magold & J. E. Carnaghi (Eds.), *Job one: Experiences of new professionals in student affairs* (pp. 59–76). Lanham, MD: University Press of America.

PBS. (n.d.). John Gardner: Engineer of the great society. Retrieved from http://www.pbs.org/johngardner/chapters/4.html

Introduction

HOW DO YOU make important decisions? Some people rely on instinct, while others may prefer a tried-and-true process. Gut decisions are most often made in moments of crisis, when there is no opportunity to weigh and calculate possible outcomes. In these and other instances, intuition can be important in decision making. However, Buchanan and O'Connell (2006) noted that "few decision makers ignore good information when they get it" (p. 41). We, the authors, contend that effective decision makers do more than solicit information; they follow a systematic set of steps to solve problems. It is by learning and practicing informed and reflective decision making that seasoned professionals develop what is commonly referred to as intuition.

In a paper on intuitive decision making submitted to the Naval War College, McCown (2010) described the case of U.S. Marine Corps General James N. Mattis, who had less than a minute to decide how to address a possible terrorist operation disguised as a wedding party during Operation Enduring Freedom. In approximately 30 seconds, using the limited intelligence available, Mattis made the decision to move in. At first glance, this example might reinforce the use of gut instinct to make quick decisions, especially when information and time are limited. However, when he was asked how long it took him to make the decision, Mattis replied, "About 30 years" (McCown, 2010, p. 1). The general's response suggests that effective decision making is a learned process, one that takes years to develop. It also suggests that with experience and training, people can become more confident in their ability to make intuitive decisions effectively. In three decades of military training, Mattis learned and practiced the highly structured Military Decision Making Process

(MDMP) (U.S. Department of the Army, 2010) and witnessed scores of senior officers make decisions. Thus, his 30-second gut decision was the culmination of a 30-year learning process.

Leaders in higher education can be said to be using intuition when they make effective (or not so effective) decisions. However, we contend that, like Mattis, student affairs practitioners develop a personalized decision-making process over the course of many years. If you are reading this book, you are most likely in the early stages of your journey as a student affairs professional, and you might be looking for guidance on how to make effective decisions. In the pages that follow, we present a decision-making framework (DMF) and case studies that will help you learn and practice how to make decisions so you can begin to develop a style of your own.

As you will see in chapter 1, little literature is available that teaches student affairs professionals how to make decisions. Emerging professionals often learn to make decisions by talking with more seasoned professionals, practicing standard operating procedures, or just plain trial and error. As educators and practitioners, we were not satisfied with such nonsystematic methods—decision making is far too important. Effective decisions can promote student development, improve practice, and gain you the respect of colleagues and supervisors. Ineffective decisions, on the other hand, can inhibit student development, detract from good practice, put you or your institution at risk for a lawsuit, and even result in bodily injury or death. The ability to make effective decisions is an integral part of sound student affairs practice and should not be left to trial and error.

In the field of student affairs, we often do not talk about *how* decisions get made. Instead, we talk about good solutions and bad decisions. Rarely do we invite emerging professionals to systematically consider how they make decisions. *Decisions Matter* offers readers an opportunity to consider both the process and the products of decision making. We propose a DMF that student affairs professionals can use to work through problems in contemporary higher education. By learning and applying the DMF to case studies and real-world problems, novice student affairs professionals can begin their journey toward developing a consistent, comprehensive, and thoughtful process for decision making. Just as Mattis developed his intuition by learning and practicing the MDMP, emerging professionals can begin to develop an intuitive decision-making style of their own by learning and practicing the framework presented in this book.

Origins of the Book

The goal of this case study book is to examine the nature of the challenges student affairs practitioners face in their daily work and offer novice professionals a framework to use for guidance in solving problems. *Decisions Matter* focuses on simulated learning experiences and the development of professional competencies. The conversation that inspired the book occurred during a faculty summit at the 2009 NASPA Region I Conference in Newport, Rhode Island. The summit convened New England regional faculty and senior student affairs officers to talk about improving the way graduate programs prepare new practitioners. One of the critical issues raised was the need for faculty to better prepare graduate students to address real-world problems. The senior student affairs officers and faculty in attendance agreed that a collection of contemporary case studies would help faculty prepare students to respond effectively to modern student affairs dilemmas. Less seasoned professionals often have a solid foundation in theory but little real-life experience making tough decisions. When they encounter crises or problems, new professionals can describe how theories inform practice, but they often are unfamiliar with the steps that must be taken to effectively solve complex problems.

Many faculty members expressed their belief that the ratio of simulated learning experiences (e.g., case studies and classroom activities) to theory-based lectures was disproportionate in many graduate preparation programs. A number of them admitted that because they had been out of administration for many years, they were not familiar with the realities of everyday practice. They agreed that a contemporary case study book could be an effective vehicle for introducing cutting-edge problems into graduate preparation coursework and helping faculty link these real-world problems to effective decision making.

A Decision-Making Framework

A unique component of this case study book is that it provides a decision-making framework for addressing various problems, crises, challenges, and issues that educators face every day at colleges and universities. We created the framework to help graduate students and new professionals develop necessary and tangible decision-making skills to use in working through both case studies and real-world problems. We view the DMF as a toolkit practitioners can use as they make important decisions concerning both minor incidents and major crises.

Drawing from literature, professional experience, and pilot research, the DMF guides professionals through four phases of decision making. Developed with higher education and student affairs practitioners in mind, the framework can be used both as a way of thinking about the problem-solving process and as a tool for guiding that process. Because it can be used in the classroom setting as well as in real-life environments, the DMF is versatile and useful to novice and seasoned professionals alike.

USING CASE STUDIES TO PRACTICE DECISION MAKING

Using case studies in the classroom has long been a popular and effective method for teaching college students. Many academic disciplines and fields of study draw on case studies to engage students in problem-solving activities that are intended to stimulate thinking. Perhaps the most significant application of the case study method in college and university settings occurs in professional schools (e.g., law, medicine, education, and business), whose programs traditionally prepare students—both undergraduate and graduate—for careers. The applied nature of these programs requires that students become both knowledgeable and skilled in their work. The learning outcomes in applied academic programs reflect students' abilities to develop a firm knowledge base in the area under study as well as the ability to put core tenets of this knowledge to work in everyday life.

Nowhere is this more important than in the field of student affairs. The higher education landscape includes both theoretical and applied programs. While an individual graduate preparation program might be strongly identified as being one or the other, virtually all programs prepare practitioners for work in the field; thus, they incorporate learning components that address both theory and practice. The art of using theory to inform practice is one of the central values of the student affairs profession and a key philosophical component of most graduate preparation programs.

The case study method can be an important tool to help students translate theory into work and vice versa. Teaching through the use of case studies in the classroom has long been a popular and effective method for faculty to socialize students into the workplace. Although they are not a proxy for real-life problems, simulated learning experiences are powerful in that they can closely approximate such events and allow students the opportunity to solve problems in a controlled environment.

In a complex and ever-changing world, graduate students and new professionals must have opportunities to practice decision making in situations that reflect these complexities. To address this need, we issued a call for contemporary case study submissions to student affairs professionals via professional listservs and announcements at conferences. We received 31 case submissions, many of which we used in this book. (See the list of case study contributors following the acknowledgments at the front of the book.) In an effort to offer case studies that addressed a variety of topics, professional competencies, and functional areas, we augmented these submissions with newly crafted cases that reflect recent incidents experienced by the four authors, our students, and colleagues.

Many case study books are available, but we believe this one is unique. First, the cases are all rooted in reality, not in someone's imagination. As you work through the cases in this book, be assured that a student affairs professional recently dealt with a similar problem. Thus, your exploration is more than an academic exercise using a fictitious example; rather, it is preparation for the real world of student affairs work.

Second, *Decisions Matter* is different from case study books that focus on particular types of cases (e.g., ethics, diversity). Some case study books offer a range of scenarios followed by a hefty dose of theory-to-practice considerations, while others provide discussion questions, with little direction about what readers should take away from the exercise. With limited exceptions (e.g., Levy & Kozoll, 1998), case study books in higher education rarely offer a detailed description of *how* to make tough decisions. In fact, very little instruction exists on the process of decision making for student affairs professionals. *Decisions Matter* provides readers with a decision-making framework they can use to analyze an array of contemporary case studies and real-world problems.

Third, the cases in this book are contemporary. They reflect the changing landscape of higher education policy, practice, and technology. Perhaps one of the most pressing aspects of event and crisis management in contemporary higher education is the influence of technology. Technology has the power to initiate, facilitate, ameliorate, or exacerbate the progress of any event and its outcome or resolution. Decision making in our current professional, campus, and global environments requires consideration of the influence of emerging technological tools. Technology's potential for both perpetrating and resolving problems cannot be underestimated; hence, many of the case studies in this book reflect the complicated nature of technology.

Fourth, this book offers graduate students and new professionals a vehicle to master key professional competencies while making decisions about contemporary student affairs problems. *Decisions Matter* will help you learn how to make effective decisions while simultaneously reflecting on your professional competencies. We believe that a dual focus on effective decision making and competency development is paramount to the success of all student affairs professionals.

PROFESSIONAL COMPETENCIES

Many scholars and practitioners have attempted to formulate and measure professional competencies for student affairs professionals. A number of researchers (Burkard, Cole, Ott, & Stoflet, 2005; Hoffman & Bresciani, 2012; Lovell & Kosten, 2000) have identified essential knowledge, skills, and dispositions for student affairs professionals. While some have assessed seasoned professionals' perceptions of the competency levels of entry-level practitioners (see, e.g., Herdlein, 2004), others have surveyed professionals directly (Cuyjet, Longwell-Grice, & Molina, 2009; Waple, 2006). Despite the information gleaned from this research, viewpoints still differ as to which competencies are most important for novice professionals to acquire; for example, some research studies (Dickerson, Hoffman, Anan, et al., 2011; Kuk, Cobb, & Forrest, 2007) have documented the divergent opinions between faculty and senior student affairs officers.

In 2010, in an effort to generate a set of professional competencies, ACPA–College Student Educators International and NASPA–Student Affairs Administrators in Higher Education created a joint task force to identify major professional competency areas and outline expectations for professionals in the field. The resulting document was *Professional Competency Areas for Student Affairs Practitioners* (ACPA & NASPA, 2010).

In the introduction, the task force explained, "This set of Professional Competency Areas is intended to define the broad professional knowledge, skills, and, in some cases, attitudes expected of student affairs professionals regardless of their area of specialization or positional role within the field" (p. 3). The 10 professional competency areas are (1) advising and helping; (2) assessment, evaluation, and research; (3) equity, diversity, and inclusion; (4) ethical professional practice; (5) history, philosophy, and values; (6) human and organizational resources; (7) law, policy, and governance; (8) leadership; (9) personal foundations; and (10) student learning and development. Each area has basic, intermediate, and advanced outcomes. As you peruse the professional competency areas, identify those in which you are most confident and those in which you might need some professional development. How did your graduate preparation program help you acquire professional competencies? By what other means might you acquire the knowledge, skills, and attitudes described in the competency areas?

As professionals make effective (and not so effective) decisions, they should take the opportunity to reflect on and develop their professional competencies. For this reason, we crafted the cases in this book and the DMF itself around the professional competency areas—we believe that all 10 of the competency areas can be applied to each of the case studies. To help you develop skills and knowledge in certain competency areas, we discuss selected competencies in chapter 4; however, we strongly encourage you to be attuned to developing skills in *all* competency areas. Thus, we charge you with the task of extending our limited competency analyses to include your own discussions about additional competency areas, and we encourage you to use *Professional Competency Areas for Student Affairs Practitioners* as a companion reference to this book.

Regardless of when or how professionals enter the field of student affairs, they are expected to possess basic competencies in all areas, and they are encouraged to develop intermediate and advanced competencies as they progress through their careers. Professionals gain and hone their competencies through a variety of formal means, including graduate preparation programs, professional development workshops, conferences, and in-service training. In our field, we also expect much learning and growth to take place through practice. In graduate preparation programs, theory-to-practice typically takes place through internships and practicum experiences, in which novice professionals are offered continuous feedback on their developing competencies. Such educational efforts are most effective when new professionals are given space and time to critically reflect on the effectiveness of their practice. Through the reflection process, professionals not only can assess the success of their efforts but also have an opportunity to consider their decision-making process and professional competencies. As you will see in chapter 2, the DMF is composed of a series of questions to inspire reflection, and it concludes with an emphasis on assessing both the process and the outcomes of your decision making.

Because *Decisions Matter* is intended for novice professionals, the scenarios described in the case studies were selected with basic and some intermediate professional competencies in mind. The cases reflect situations that entry-level student affairs professionals might face. More complex organizational problems, which are often the purview of middle managers and senior leaders, are not included in the case studies.

The case studies in this book give you an opportunity to practice decision making and reflect on your basic and intermediate competencies in each of the 10 competency areas. For instance, in "Conduct Unbecoming" you are asked to use the DMF to address a situation between a student veteran and his roommate. Once you have worked through your decision-making process, you can turn to the Competencies Matter section, where we direct your attention to the intersections of the case study with specific professional competency areas. You are encouraged to consider how situations such as the one presented in the "Conduct Unbecoming" scenario enable you to develop and reflect on your advising and helping, and student learning and development competencies. We draw your attention to the advising and helping competency area basic-level skill to "actively seek out opportunities to expand one's own knowledge and skills in helping students with specific concerns (e.g., suicidal students) as well as interfacing with specific populations within the college environment (e.g., student veterans)" (ACPA & NASPA, 2010, p. 6). We then invite you to assess your level of competency. How would you describe your knowledge and skills in working with student veterans? If you feel exceptionally competent in this area, you might decide to focus on developing other competencies. If you think you need more knowledge and skills to effectively work with student veterans, you might want to focus on this competency.

In the brief discussion that follows each case, we direct your attention to selected resources that might be useful to help you increase your knowledge. The suggestions are not meant to be prescriptive or all-inclusive; they represent a small slice of the available resources. We hope these suggestions will inspire you to consider the endless ways to increase your professional competencies. For instance, you might participate in a webinar, attend a conference session, read a book or journal article about student veteran issues, or conduct your own field work by talking to veterans and veterans affairs experts. The avenues to increase your competencies are endless. This is the beauty of competency development: It is professional work framed as a personal endeavor. Given the multitude of opportunities for professional growth, you can choose professional development methods that match your preferred learning style. This personalized perspective on competency development is summarized in *Professional Competency Areas for Student Affairs Practitioners* as follows:

> If student affairs professionals desire to grow in a particular competency area, they can examine expected learning and skills in the intermediate and advanced levels. Such examination allows individual practitioners to use this document to help guide their own choices about professional development opportunities afforded to them. (ACPA & NASPA, 2010, p. 3)

We agree with that statement and encourage you to use *Decisions Matter* in conjunction with *Professional Competency Areas for Student Affairs Practitioners* to personally tailor your professional development.

How to Use *Decisions Matter*

Decisions Matter was crafted with multiple audiences in mind. First, the book can be used by graduate preparation program faculty and students. The use of case studies for teaching and learning is endemic to the student affairs field, because it facilitates the practical application of theoretical perspectives. It can easily be coupled with the practicum component of many higher education and student affairs programs, where the training of future professionals is crucial. Additionally, the cases address each of the 10 professional competencies and a wide range of issues and functional areas, so *Decisions Matter* can be used to augment almost any course in a graduate preparation program. For instance, cases such as "Fraternities and Faith," "Brianna's Boyfriend," and "Can I Help?" provide scenarios ripe for discussion in a helping skills course. Professors and students who are exploring issues of cultural competency and diversity might find "Care for Maria," "Sally's Situation," or "Honor Thy Father and Thy Mother" especially applicable. More than a third of the case studies relate to issues of law and governance and could be used to augment traditional policy or organizational governance texts. Because of its applicability to a variety of aspects of student affairs work, faculty might consider adopting *Decisions Matter* as a program resource to be used across the curriculum or as a supplemental text for a particular course. So that educators can easily find cases that match specific pedagogical needs, a list is provided at the end of the book where cases are organized by competency area, institutional type, department/functional area, and topic.

This book can also be used by student affairs departments that employ graduate assistants or host graduate student interns. All supervisors want their graduate students to make good decisions. To that end, many student affairs offices dedicate a substantial amount of time and other resources to providing pre-service and in-service training to graduate employees. *Decisions Matter* can be paired with department-specific training about office culture, ethics in the workplace, department protocols, and employee expectations. Using the DMF and case studies can help graduate assistants not only learn the theory but also practice how to make effective decisions in department-specific contexts.

Decisions Matter extends the work of graduate preparation programs in developing new professionals and thus can also be used as a professional development tool. Student affairs is a broad-based profession, and no graduate preparation program can sufficiently cover all the topics, issues, and concerns that face the field. This can be both a blessing and a curse, as entry-, middle-, and even senior-level student affairs professionals are often asked to step into situations on the basis of an assumption that they have knowledge when, in fact, they may have little experience. Such is the nature of a broadly defined profession that encompasses a variety of disparate functional areas. Professionals are expected to be knowledgeable about an entire field and have skills that are transferable to a host of functional areas. The case studies in this book simulate experiences that you might never have but which might prove invaluable to your training. Such practice is good for professionals in almost any stage of a student affairs career. Because the DMF and the case studies in this book are tied to the *Professional Competency Areas for Student Affairs Practitioners*, any student affairs department or division could infuse this volume into professional development sessions. We suggest that supervisors of early career professionals consider using the DMF and selected case studies during in-service training or for individualized skill development. In addition, the case studies can be used with entire departments and divisions. Having entry- and mid-level professionals work collaboratively on case studies can be educational for all parties involved. During one of our pilot sessions, mid-level and novice student affairs professionals worked in cross-level groups to apply the DMF to sample cases. The ensuing conversations were enlightening for both groups.

STRUCTURE OF THE BOOK

In the following pages, you have an opportunity to learn about a decision-making framework that was vetted by a variety of student affairs professionals. But first we offer you a glimpse into the literature on decision making. Chapter 1 provides a brief review of decision making from higher education, business, military, medical, and social science literature. We summarize a variety of decision-making models, but note that none are perfectly suited for decisions faced by entry-level student affairs professionals. In chapter 2, we introduce you to our own decision-making framework, which was designed for novice practitioners and pilot-tested by graduate students and a variety of professionals who supervise graduate assistants (i.e., entry- and mid-level professionals). After giving a brief history of the development of the DMF, we describe the four phases and the key questions and considerations for each phase. Chapter 3 provides a sample case study. In that chapter, we offer readers a phase-by-phase example of how the DMF can be used to work through a case study. Chapter 4 is composed of 30 case studies. Because the DMF focuses on context and competencies, each case study is followed by a series of questions labeled Context Matters. In this section, we invite you to revisit your decision-making process in light of three or four hypothetical changes to the case study context. After you have an opportunity to reconsider your decision in light of the changing context, we ask you to consider which professional competencies were most closely related to the case study. As you work through the cases, you will no doubt recognize that most can be connected to the majority of the professional competencies. Instead of reviewing the applicability of each competency area to every case, we suggest two or three competency areas that could be salient to the scenario. Thus, the Competencies Matter discussions are not meant to be a comprehensive review of the relevant competencies—that discussion is beyond the scope of this book. Instead, the Competencies Matter discussion for each case is intended to ignite your reflection on the professional competency areas. As you endeavor to become a well-rounded and competent professional, we encourage you to consider how the 10 competency areas relate to each case study and how your responses reflect your current competency level. A list of cases organized by competency area, institutional type, department/ functional area, and topic is included at the end of the book. Finally, *Decisions Matter* includes a color insert that summarizes the DMF. We encourage you to utilize the insert as you navigate cases in this book and real-life situations.

REFERENCES

American College Personnel Association (ACPA) and National Association of Student Personnel Administrators (NASPA). (2010). *Professional competency areas for student affairs practitioners.* Retrieved from http://www.naspa.org/programs/prodev/Professional_Competencies.pdf

Buchanan, L., & O'Connell, A. (2006). A brief history of decision making. *Harvard Business Review, 84*(1), 32–41.

Burkard, A. W., Cole, D. C., Ott, M., & Stoflet, T. (2005). Entry-level competencies of new professionals: A Delphi study. *Journal of Student Affairs Research and Practice, 42*(3), 283–309.

Cuyjet, M. J., Longwell-Grice, R., & Molina, E. (2009). Perceptions of new student affairs professionals and their supervisors regarding the application of competencies learned in preparation programs. *Journal of College Student Development, 50*(1), 104–119.

Dickerson, A. M., Hoffman, J. L., Anan, B. P., Brown, K. F., Vong, L. K., Bresciani, M. J., Monzon, R., & Hickmott, J. (2011). A comparison of senior student affairs officers and student affairs preparatory faculty expectations of entry-level professionals' competencies. *Journal of Student Affairs Research and Practice, 48*(4), 463–479.

Herdlein, R. J., III. (2004). Survey of chief student affairs officers regarding relevance of graduate preparation of new professionals. *NASPA Journal, 42*(1), 51–70.

Hoffman, J. L., & Bresciani, M. J. (2012). Identifying what student affairs professionals value: A mixed methods analysis of professional competencies listed in job descriptions. *Research and Practice in Assessment, 7,* 26–40.

Kuk, L., Cobb, B., & Forrest, C. (2007). Perceptions of competencies of entry-level practitioners in student affairs. *NASPA Journal,* *44*(4), 664–691.

Levy, S. R., & Kozoll, C. E. (1998). *A guide to decision making in student affairs: A case study approach.* Springfield, IL: C. C. Thomas.

Lovell, C. D., & Kosten, L. A. (2000). Skills, knowledge, and personal traits necessary for success as a student affairs administrator: A meta-analysis of thirty years of research. *NASPA Journal,* *37*(4), 353–369.

McCown, N. R. (2010). *Developing intuitive decision-making in modern military leadership.* [Paper submitted to the faculty of the Naval War College.] Retrieved from http://www.au.af.mil/au/awc/awcgate/navy/nwc_mccown.pdf

U.S. Department of the Army. (2010). *The operations process* (field manual 5-0). Retrieved from http://www.fas.org/irp/doddir/army/fm5-0.pdf

Waple, J. N. (2006). An assessment of skills and competencies necessary for entry-level student affairs work. *NASPA Journal, 43*(1), 1–18.

CHAPTER 1

Decision-Making Literature

WE BELIEVE THAT developing effective decision-making skills in the workplace is both an art and a science. We also contend that decision making is both a process and a product. Our perceptions align with those of Zeleny (1982), who suggested two approaches to decision making: (1) the outcomes-oriented approach, which is informed by the notion that "if one can correctly predict the outcome of the decision process, then one obviously understands the decision process" (p. 85); and (2) the process-oriented approach, which holds the view that "if one understands the decision process, one can correctly predict the outcome" (p. 85). People are most often remembered for the outcome or product of their decision making. A quick scan of the higher education news reveals an array of stories describing the outcomes of poor decisions, but almost never do we read about the process that practitioners used to make those decisions. *Decisions Matter* offers you an opportunity to consider both the process and the outcomes of decision making.

1

What makes a decision effective, ineffective, or disastrous? Most people look at the outcome, but the process can be equally important. Sometimes we learn to make decisions by thinking in reverse— engaging in what Weick (1995) called "retrospective sensemaking." That is, we examine events in retrospect and begin to more deeply understand the various actions we took along the way and why we took them. Many practitioners, new and seasoned alike, go through this process every day when they are confronted with problem situations in the work environment. While we hope that you will learn from each of your professional decisions, we do not recommend relying solely on retrospective sensemaking. Instead, we believe that to be an effective practitioner, you must learn from both the outcomes of your decisions and the process you used to arrive at those decisions.

LITERATURE

We present a snapshot of the interdisciplinary literature on decision making that provides some context for the creation and development of our own model. Numerous decision-making models, theories, and guides exist in higher education, business, psychology, military, medical, and organizational literature. Among the array of options available to practitioners, graduate program directors, and faculty members, we sought to determine which, if any, would be most useful for entry-level student affairs professionals. As we developed our decision-making framework (DMF) for new student affairs professionals, we consulted classic and contemporary literature and found that the topic of decision making was primarily the domain of the organizational behavior and business management fields (Cohen, March, & Olsen, 1972; Dean & Sharfman, 1996; March & Simon, 1958; Mintzberg, Raisinghani, &

Theoret, 1976; Zeleny, 1982). We also found a significant amount of research in the social sciences that focused on inter- and intrapersonal aspects of decision making and the cognitive processes used in decision making (Capelo & Dias, 2009; Eggert & Bogeholz, 2010; Janis, 1982; Roets & Van Hiel, 2011; Schwenk, 1984), as well as the role of culture in decision processes (Frame & Williams, 2005; Hays, Prosek, & McLeod, 2010; Park & DeShon, 2010). The military and medical fields offered insight into the need to balance strategic and intuitive decision making (Chapman & Sonnenberg, 2000; Charles, Gafni, & Whelan, 1997, 1999; Knighton, 2004; McCown, 2010; Roberts & Sonnenberg, 2000; Sonnenberg & Beck, 2008; U.S. Department of the Army, 2010). Finally, legal and political references contributed to our understanding of decision-making processes and outcomes (Drobak & North, 2008; Posner, 1988; Simon, 2004; Terwel, Harinck, Ellemers, & Daamen, 2010).

In addition to literature on general decision making, related bodies of literature describe ethical decision making in business and higher education, which we found instructive and useful for the development of our cases (Anderson & Davies, 2000; Baird, 2005; Ferrell & Gresham, 1985; Frame & Williams, 2005; Fried, 2011; Humphrey, Janosik, & Creamer, 2004; Hunt & Vitell, 1986; Jones, 1991; Kocet, McCauley, & Thompson, 2009; Mitchell & Yordy, 2010; Nash, 2002; Rogerson, Gottlieb, Handelsman, Knapp, & Younggren, 2011).

In the following pages, we highlight some of the classic and contemporary works on decision making, noting their applicability and shortcomings for student affairs use. This chapter is not intended to provide a comprehensive review of the literature—entire volumes are dedicated to such reviews. Rather, it provides a snapshot of the ways scholars and practitioners from a variety of disciplines and professions view decision making. While literature in each of these domains has something valuable to offer, none of them provides an ideal roadmap for novice student affairs professionals navigating complicated campus dilemmas. Thus, after an in-depth review of the literature, we saw a need for a framework that would guide novice student affairs professionals through the decision-making process.

Is Decision Making Rational?

Much of the classic decision literature focuses on rational decision making. The concept of rationality assumes that people make decisions in the context of clearly defined environments. Rationality also suggests that decision makers engage in an orderly process through which they conduct a logical cognitive analysis of the pros and cons of a situation, then select what they believe to be the optimal solution to a problem. Many classic and contemporary decision-making models reflect this rational paradigm. For instance, Knighton (2004) noted that the military's "primary decision-making tool—the estimate process—is based on the rational model of decision making" (p. 309). Similarly, many legal scholars argue that decision making in our legal system, particularly by judges, is based on rationality; that is, "the judge is a rational actor who reasons logically from facts, previous decisions, statues, and constitutions to reach a decision" (Drobak & North, 2008, p. 131). Logic and direct interpretation of the law direct legal action. Conversely, the legal realists, who align themselves with the writings of Oliver Wendell Holmes Jr., believe that "the life of the law" (Holmes, 1881, p. 1) must reflect the needs of the people, place, and times. In essence, the rules can and should change as needed, and it is the duty of the decision maker to think beyond what is prescribed to become a contemporary interpreter of the law.

Like legal realists, classic and contemporary organizational, business, and education scholars recognize the shortcomings of strict notions of rationality. In their classic text *Organizations*, March and Simon (1958) explicate a variety of limits to rationality, such as incomplete information, poor communication, differences in individual and organizational goals, time pressures, attention span, and personal discretion. Concerns about time, limited information, and the capacity of the human brain to envision and analyze all possible solutions have led decision-making literature to focus on bounded rationality as opposed to strict rationality. In such models, decision makers are bounded (i.e., constrained) by limits such as time, available information, and cognitive capacity. In a system of bounded rationality, a person chooses among limited or incomplete options to arrive at a satisfactory versus an optimal or ideal solution (Simon, 1982).

Some scholars, however, argue that any form of rationality—ideal, bounded, or otherwise—cannot adequately account for the complexities and nonrational processes used by humans and organizations as they engage in decision making. Even Knighton (2004)—who described military decision making as rooted in rationality—admitted that cognitive shortcuts, personality factors, organizational culture, personal assessments of risk, and the complexity of real-life situations lead military personnel to regularly violate the principles of rationality in decision-making processes. Similarly, Zeleny (1982) asserted that decision making is anything but purely systematic and rational when he described the process as "a complex search for information, full of detours, enriched by feedback from casting about in all directions, gathering and discarding information, fueled by fluctuating uncertainty, indistinct and conflicting concepts—some sharp, some hazy" (p. 86). In an article about group decision making, Kacprzyk, Fedrizzi, and Nurmi (1992) explained how fuzzy logic can influence decision making. One of the most striking concepts refuting careful and calculated decision making is referred to as "garbage can decision making" (Cohen et al., 1972). In their research on higher education organizations, Cohen et al. wrote:

> The garbage can process is one in which problems, solutions, and participants move from one choice opportunity to another in such a way that the nature of the choice, the time it takes, and the problem it solves all depend on a relatively complicated intermeshing of elements. These include the mix of choices available at any one time, the mix of problems that have access to the organization, the mix of solutions looking for problems, and the outside demands on decision makers. (p. 16)

They noted that higher education decision making (including the nature of problems and solutions) is not simplistic, nor does it follow a linear, rational process.

In an analysis of the debate about whether legal decision making is rational or not, Simon (2004) argued that "neither account is completely convincing" (p. 512). We, too, believe that neither rational models nor alternative models of decision making are perfect. Although we realize that problem-solving and decision-making activities are not always clear or conducted in a rational manner, we contend that a *somewhat* rational framework provides necessary structure for novice decision makers. Thus, we created a decision-making framework (DMF) that contains phases and questions that reflect a model of bounded rationality. Each phase flows logically from the previous one, and every question invites practitioners to develop possible options and then choose the best one. In short, the phases and questions in the DMF reflect a rational paradigm. However, we acknowledge that bounded rationality can be interpreted in various ways by different organizations and that logical flow to one person or constituency might be illogical to another.

But the DMF is not solely about a lock-step hierarchical system and purely rational choices. Student affairs professionals are often faced with a variety of surprises, unclear situations, and changing conditions. Our DMF is designed so that at any point the decision maker can return to a previous phase. The DMF is less linear than it is iterative. Humans are imperfect beings whose life histories, professional experiences, unique personalities, developmental locations, and risk-taking propensities influence their decisions. Moreover, decision making in student affairs exists within campus, community, and societal contexts. As you will see in chapter 2, the seemingly rational phases and questions in the DMF are bound by contexts that can lead a professional to make nonoptimal or nonrational decisions. For instance, an emerging professional may feel pressured by political influences on campus to make a decision that he or she deems less than optimal. Or a novice professional may work at a campus bounded by unique town-gown relationships and thus may make decisions based on these relationships rather than selecting rational options that solely benefit the campus. In sum, the DMF offers novice professionals a framework that is rooted in bounded rationality but acknowledges the complicated contextual issues that regularly lead to less than rational (e.g., optimal) decisions.

HIGHLIGHTS FROM THE LITERATURE

Scholars and practitioners have long searched for ways to understand the decision-making process. Indeed, many step or stage models explain the process of how individuals, groups, and organizations make effective decisions. Some of this literature focuses on the process

(Baird, 2005; Zeleny, 1982) while some focuses on the effectiveness of decision-making outcomes (Dean & Sharfman, 1996). In the following paragraphs, we offer a snapshot of selected literature on decision-making processes and briefly note how each can be useful (or not so useful) to student affairs work. First, we describe general models of individual, group, and organizational decision making. Quite a bit of scholarly writing addresses effective higher education leadership or organizational effectiveness, but our review of the literature yielded only one commonly cited general decision-making model created for higher education professionals (Levy & Kozoll, 1998). After an overview of general decision-making models, we review a subset of the literature that focuses exclusively on ethical decision making. Since contemporary student affairs problems sometimes have an ethical component, we would be remiss if we did not include such models. While some higher education scholars and practitioners have wrestled with ethical decision making in higher education and student affairs (Fried, 2011; Humphrey et al., 2004; Kocet et al., 2009; Nash, 2002), many ethical decision-making models originate from outside the educational realm. Following this summary of classic and contemporary decision-making processes, we turn our attention to decision-making effectiveness.

How do individuals, groups, and organizations make decisions? Great thinkers have pondered that question for centuries. Buchanan and O'Connell (2006) provided a lengthy timeline of human beings making decisions throughout history. In prehistoric times, decisions were often influenced by smoke, dreams, or oracles. In the sixth century BC, the ancient Chinese teacher and philosopher Confucius taught that decisions should be informed by benevolence, ritual, reciprocity, and filial piety (Buchanan & O'Connell, 2006). In the seventeenth century, English and French philosophers such as Francis Bacon and René Descartes believed that scientific reasoning should undergird the decision-making process. In the nineteenth and twentieth centuries, organizational and business leaders viewed logical issues of risk, probability, and individual/organizational interests as central aspects of decision making. Such perspectives are in striking contrast to the psychoanalytic theorist Sigmund Freud's perspective that decisions are partly influenced by our unconscious (Buchanan & O'Connell, 2006).

In this chapter we stick to contemporary (and mostly U.S.-based) ideas about decision making. We cannot provide a comprehensive review of all decision-making models in this short chapter. Instead, the following paragraphs provide a glimpse into the various ways decisions are believed to be made in contemporary society. These works reflect the ways educators, legal scholars, military personnel, medical professionals, and organizational thinkers have wrestled with the task of making sense of decision-making processes and outcomes.

A classic work from the business field by Mintzberg et al. (1976) analyzed the decision-making processes of 25 organizations and summarized those processes into three phases: identification, development, and selection. The identification phase includes recognition that a crisis exists and a decision must be made, as well as a diagnosis of the causes and effects of the problem (pp. 252–253). In the development phase, decision makers may search for "ready-made solutions" or design new solutions (p. 255). In the selection phase, the available solutions are screened and evaluated. Once a course of action is chosen, decision makers seek authorization or approval from superiors in the organization. Due to the general nature of the process described by Mintzberg et al., it can be used by any decision maker, including those in student affairs. However, what is missing in this work is an intentional reflection on both the process and the outcomes of decision making.

To summarize and simplify various decision-making processes, Schwenk (1984) elucidated the similarities among four classic strategic decision-making models. In his efforts to synthesize these four models (Glueck, 1976; Hofer & Schendel, 1978; Mazzolini, 1981; Mintzberg et al., 1976), Schwenk constructed a new model, which simplified decision making to a four-step process: (1) formulation of goals and identification of problems; (2) generation of strategic alternatives; (3) evaluation and selection of possible solutions; and (4) implementation.

While Schwenk was intent on simplifying decision-making models, Zeleny (1982) offered a much lengthier 16-stage decision-making process. In this extended model, each decision stage is highlighted by a predecision in which the person experiences cognitive dissonance surrounding the suitable (or less than suitable) options. Zeleny argued that people make partial decisions throughout the decision-making process as opposed to one grand decision. Argyris (1976) agreed that "complex decisions can be subdivided and the subordinate problems solved in some sort of functional sequence" (p. 365). The notion of partial or multiple sequential decisions can be useful to novice professionals. Contemporary student affairs problems are complex; rarely do they involve a single decision. Instead, professionals are faced with a series of small decisions as they proceed through the decision-making process. Real-world situations require professionals to decide what the problem actually is, what the options are, which option is best, and how to implement solutions. While the ideas from business and organizational science can be useful to student affairs professionals, the generic nature of these classic works may leave new student affairs decision makers wanting more.

One of the most frequently cited decision-making resources for business, particularly in the area of marketing, is the SWOT (strengths, weaknesses, opportunities, and threats) analysis. The original SWOT framework was developed in the 1960s by Edmund Learned, C. Roland Christensen, Kenneth Andrews, and others, and later expanded upon by Albert Humphrey (Buchanan & O'Connell, 2006). A SWOT model of analysis does not lead a person through a series of decision-making steps; however, it allows a person to make an informed decision after filtering through a concise list of strengths, weaknesses, opportunities, and threats. A SWOT analysis can be particularly useful when circumstances are complicated and when decisions need to be made quickly. While SWOT analyses focus on strengths, weaknesses, opportunities, and threats to an organization, a PEST (political, economic, social, and technological) analysis offers an additional tool to analyze the external environment. Higher education organizations must deal with an ever-changing and fast-paced external macro-environment, and they have learned to respond quickly. It is common for a PEST analysis to be done in tandem with a SWOT analysis. Both the SWOT and PEST analyses, however, have been criticized for oversimplifying situations and underestimating the complexity of environmental factors. Individuals and groups in higher education organizations may need more detailed tools to solve contemporary student affairs problems. Assessing strengths, weaknesses, opportunities, and threats should certainly inform decision-making processes. However, SWOT analyses do not offer much insight about how to proceed once the analysis is complete, nor do they require decision makers to engage in much reflection.

The military, on the other hand, requires its personnel to use a highly structured and collaborative decision-making process called the Military Decision Making Process (MDMP). *The Operations Process* (U.S. Department of the Army, 2010) described it as "an iterative planning methodology that integrates the activities of the commander, staff, subordinate headquarters, and other partners to understand the situation and mission; develop and compare courses of action; decide on a course of action that best accomplishes a mission; and produce an operation plan or order for execution" (p. B-1). The MDMP begins with receipt of the mission from headquarters. Once the mission is received, a decision maker proceeds through six steps: (1) mission analysis, (2) course of action (COA) development, (3) COA analysis, (4) COA comparison, (5) COA approval, and (6) orders production. Each step has key inputs and outputs. Continuous assessment is at the heart of military decision making: "It precedes and guides every operations process activity and concludes each operation or phase of an operation" (U.S. Department of the Army, 2010, p. 6-1). While some concepts in this model (e.g., receipt of mission) might seem irrelevant to student affairs, other parts (e.g., analysis and comparison of potential courses of action) are behaviors in which student affairs decision makers regularly engage.

The medical field also has a multitude of decision-making models for diagnosis and treatment (Chapman & Sonnenberg, 2000; Charles et al., 1997, 1999; Roberts & Sonnenberg, 2000; Sonnenberg & Beck, 2008), and some of these have particular relevance for student affairs work. Chapman and Sonnenberg (2000) explained how medical "decision making itself is in constant evolution. Over the past twenty years, models have evolved from simple trees with 'arbitrary' (non-utility-based) outcome measures to increasingly sophisticated models . . . made possible largely through the development of sophisticated microcomputer software" (p. 15). In a review of seven decision-making techniques, Roberts and Sonnenberg (2000) suggested that despite their differences, all medical decision-making models include problem construction; understanding the context, detail, and complexity; assessment of risk; and understanding time horizons.

Medical decision making depends on a host of variables related to the patient's status (e.g., emergency treatment, treatment of chronic illness, preventive care, palliative care) and the context. A contextual variable that often shapes medical decision making is the roles doctors and patients assume, and the power associated with those roles (Charles et al., 1997). For instance, decision making in a physician-as-agent model assumes that the practitioner knows best. In such models, patients are rarely involved in decision making. Conversely, in an informed-decision-making model, the physician explains a diagnosis and all the possible treatments. Armed with this knowledge, patients engage in independent decision making about their course of treatment. Finally, in a shared treatment decision-making model, patients and doctors cooperatively engage in treatment decisions. Despite these differences, Charles et al. (1999) acknowledged that while the roles of patient and physician differ, most treatment decision-making models include similar stages: information exchange, deliberation, selecting a treatment, and implementation.

Thus far, we have discussed decision-making models from other professions, but this book was written for student affairs professionals. One of the frequently cited decision-making models available in higher education is from Levy and Kozoll (1998), whose student affairs case study book drew on the experiences of 15 senior student affairs officers to provide a resource for training new professionals and preparing graduate students for work in the field. The decision-making process developed by the authors reflected the decisions senior-level admin-istrators made with respect to a variety of issues, such as finance and budgeting, town-gown relationships, and residence life. The authors explored the complexities of day-to-day decision making, noting the importance of understanding and defining the problem, determining the context, finding necessary facts, and considering the potential reper-cussions of various decisions. They posed questions in 10 areas to help senior student affairs officers reflect on the decision-making process: (1) define the problem, (2) decide on the participants, (3) determine the background, (4) find the facts, (5) determine the local context,

(6) consider the consequences, (7) set a time frame, (8) identify superiors, (9) consider past situations, and (10) predict repercussions. Although the Levy and Kozoll model is relevant to decision making at all professional levels, we believe that novice decision makers need more specific guidance to effectively tackle complex problems.

Many of the aforementioned works relate to general decision-making processes, but some scholars have focused specifically on ethical decision making (Baird, 2005; Ferrell & Gresham, 1985; Humphrey et al., 2004; Hunt & Vitell, 1986; Kocet et al., 2009). Jones (1991) synthesized five classic ethical decision-making processes and determined that they shared five common stages or phases. First, each model situates the ethical decision-making process in an environmental (e.g., social, cultural, organizational, peer) context. Second, a person must recognize an event or issue as a moral one. Once that determination is made, the person makes some sort of moral judgment or evaluation, depending on his or her stage of moral reasoning (Gilligan, 1977; Kohlberg, 1969; Rest, 1986). Then the decision maker establishes moral intent, balancing "moral factors against other factors, notably including self-interest" (Jones, 1991, p. 386). Finally, the person acts on those moral intentions and engages in moral behavior.

Baird (2005) expanded upon the work of Lonergan (1973) to suggest five steps people use to make ethical decisions. Baird's model focused on four ethical lenses: rights/responsibility, relationship, reputation, and results. Each lens is based on a philosophical tradition. The rights and responsibility lens and the relationship lens are rooted in the deontological tradition, which focuses on issues of duty. Conversely, the goal-based teleological tradition informs the reputation and results lenses. Baird's model is useful for highlighting the various ethical lenses that can be used during decision making. When used in conjunction with ethical principles for the profession, this model can be helpful in solving ethical dilemmas.

Fried (2011) noted that among the variety of commonly accepted standards and principles in the field of student affairs, a single agreed-upon process for resolving ethical dilemmas does not exist. However, she acknowledged that "most approaches have common characteristics, such as careful data gathering, analysis, consultation, and decision making" (p. 115). Kocet et al. (2009) designed a 12-step ethical decision-making process specifically for student affairs professionals. The steps begin with the development of an ethical worldview and end with reflection on how the decision-making experience will inform future actions. Humphrey et al. (2004) put forth another ethical decision-making model for higher education; they suggested that the path to ethical decision making has four process steps: "(a) identifying the problem; (b) classifying the type of problem in ethical terms; (c) considering the relevant ethical principles, character traits, and professional values; and (d) making an ethical decision" (pp. 680–682). But not all professional problems are necessarily ethical dilemmas; thus, none of these ethical decision-making models are ideal for solving all types of contemporary student affairs problems.

A Focus on Effectiveness

In assessing the effectiveness of decision making, the emphasis should be on both process and outcomes; however, not all literature on decision making effectiveness focuses on both. For instance, much of the literature describing the roadblocks to effective decision making addresses particular aspects of the decision-making process. Some scholars have focused on premature closure, which happens when a decision is made before all possible options are considered (Easterbrook, 1959; Janis, 1982). Others have attributed ineffective decisions to temporal narrowing, which occurs when a person rushes to a solution without devoting sufficient time to considering all alternatives (Janis, 1982). In a simulation study of 100 undergraduate students, Keinan (1987) found that when people were under stress, they made decisions before they considered all alternatives. Moreover, participants did not use a systematic process to consider all possible options. We kept these pitfalls in mind in crafting our DMF. We certainly cannot control for the amount of stress you will feel as you attempt to solve contemporary student affairs problems. However, the DMF contains a series of questions that will help you avoid temporal narrowing and preclosure, and encourage you to conduct a more comprehensive scan of your options before you act.

In contrast to literature that emphasizes factors that hinder specific aspects of the decision-making process, Dean and Sharfman (1996) conducted research on the decision-making process to determine whether strategic decision making was related to decision effectiveness. This longitudinal study examined more than 50 major decisions in 24 companies to determine which factors contribute to decision-making success. Dean and Sharfman's work featured a model of strategic decision-making effectiveness defined as the "extent to which a decision achieves the objectives established by management at the time it is made" (p. 372). Their findings suggested that procedural rationality, favorable environmental conditions, and quality of implementation were significant predictors of decision-making effectiveness. Conversely, when decisions were made in a political context in which individual goals superseded organizational goals, decision-making effectiveness was negatively influenced. This work highlights the many factors that lead to decision-making effectiveness, including the extent to which effectiveness is defined by the context in which the decision is made. A decision that is effective for one department, unit, or institution may not be effective for another if the cultures and operating environments are different. Dean and Sharfman (1996) wrote that "for a decision process to result in effective choice, it must be (1) oriented toward achieving appropriate organization goals, (2) based on accurate information linking various alternatives to these goals, and (3) based on appreciation and understanding of environmental constraints" (p. 373). Thus, effective decision making is bound within the institutional context and defined by the players involved in the process. It is in that spirit that we offer our DMF, which provides a fairly linear, rationally bounded, and sequential model for evaluating problem situations in higher education. As you will see in chapter 2, the DMF is bound by the ever-changing professional, campus, and external contexts.

SUMMARY

In this chapter, we explained how decision making is both a process and a product. Effective decisions can lead to successful student and institutional outcomes, while ineffective decisions can lead to outcomes that negatively affect students, staff, and institutions. To make effective decisions, professionals must learn the process of decision making. A review of higher education, business, social science, law, medicine, and military literature yields no shortage of decision-making models. With few exceptions, most of the decision-making models presented in this chapter are intended for use by particular audiences, namely business, political, medical, or military. None of them are suited for student affairs, which is a relatively specific field in which ethical, crisis-related, and mundane issues must be solved. Models devised for business and industry or the military are a poor match for the complex interpersonal nature of student affairs work. However, little higher education literature explicitly addresses how student affairs professionals can make effective decisions, so practitioners are often forced to go outside the field for literature on decision making.

In addition, we shared a few examples of decision-making models designed for higher education professionals. While each of the models has something useful to offer, none of them are ideally suited for novice decision makers in student affairs. In the next chapter, we propose a decision-making framework specifically designed to assist graduate students and new professionals as they learn and practice the process of decision making in higher education settings.

References

Anderson, S. K., & Davies, T. (2000). An ethical decision-making model: A necessary tool for community college presidents and boards of trustees. *Community College Journal of Research and Practice, 24*(9), 711–727.

Argyris, C. (1976). Single-loop and double-loop models in research on decision making. *Administrative Science Quarterly, 21*(3), 363–375.

Baird, C. (2005). *Everyday ethics: Making hard choices in a complex world.* Centennial, CO: CB Resources.

Buchanan, L., & O'Connell, A. (2006). A brief history of decision making. *Harvard Business Review, 84*(1), 32–41.

Capelo, C., & Dias, J. (2009). A feedback learning and mental models perspective on strategic decision making. *Educational Technology Research and Development, 57*(5), 629–644.

Chapman, G. B., & Sonnenberg, F. A. (2000). Introduction. In G. B. Chapman & F. A. Sonnenberg (Eds.), *Decision making in health care: Theory, psychology and applications* (pp. 3–19). Cambridge, England: Cambridge University Press.

Charles, C., Gafni, A., & Whelan, T. (1997). Shared decision-making in the medical encounter: What does it mean? (Or, it takes at least two to tango). *Social Science and Medicine, 44*, 681–692.

Charles, C., Gafni, A., & Whelan, T. (1999). Decision-making in the physician-patient encounter: Revisiting the shared treatment decision-making model. *Social Science and Medicine, 49*, 651–661.

Cohen, M. D., March, J. D., & Olsen, J. P. (1972). A garbage can model of organizational choice. *Administrative Science Quarterly, 17*(1), 1–25.

Dean, J. W., Jr., & Sharfman, M. P. (1996). Does decision process matter? A study of strategic decision-making effectiveness. *Academy of Management Journal, 39*(2), 368–396.

Drobak, J. N., & North, D. C. (2008). Understanding judicial decision-making: The importance of constraints on non-rational deliberations. *Journal of Law and Policy, 26*, 131–152.

Easterbrook, J. A. (1959). The effect of emotion on cue utilization and organizational behavior. *Psychology Review, 66*, 183–201.

Eggert, S., & Bogeholz, S. (2010). Students' use of decision-making strategies with regard to socioscientific issues: An application of the Rasch partial credit model. *Science Education, 94*(2), 230–258.

Ferrell, O. C., & Gresham, L. (1985). A contingency framework for understanding ethical decision making in marketing. *Journal of Marketing, 49*, 87–96.

Frame, M., & Williams, C. (2005). A model of ethical decision making from a multicultural perspective. *Counseling and Values, 49*(3), 165–179.

Fried, J. (2011). Ethical standards and principles. In J. H. Schuh, S. R. Jones, & S. R. Harper (Eds.), *Student services: A handbook for the profession* (5th ed., pp. 96–119). San Francisco, CA: Jossey-Bass.

Gilligan, C. (1977). In a different voice: Women's conception of self and morality. *Harvard Educational Review, 47*, 481–517.

Glueck, W. F. (1976). *Business policy: Strategy formulation and management action*. New York, NY: McGraw-Hill.

Hays, D. G., Prosek, E. A., & McLeod, A. L. (2010). A mixed methodological analysis of the role of culture in the clinical decision-making process. *Journal of Counseling and Development, 88*(1), 114–121.

Hofer, C. W., & Schendel, D. (1978). *Strategy formulation: Analytical concepts.* St. Paul, MN: West.

Holmes, O. W. (1881). *The common law.* Boston, MA: Little Brown.

Humphrey, E., Janosik, S. M., & Creamer, D. G. (2004). The role of principles, character, and professional values in ethical decision-making. *NASPA Journal, 41*(3), 675–692.

Hunt, S. D., & Vitell, S. (1986). A general theory of marketing ethics. *Journal of Macromarketing, 6,* 5–16.

Janis, I. L. (1982). Decision making under stress. In L. Goldberger & S. Breznitz (Eds.), *Handbook of stress: Theoretical and clinical aspects* (pp. 69–80). New York, NY: Free Press.

Jones, T. M. (1991). Ethical decision making by individuals in organizations: An issue-contingent model. *Academy of Management Review, 16*(2), 366–395.

Kacprzyk, J., Fedrizzi, M., & Nurmi, H. (1992). Group decision making and consensus under fuzzy preferences and fuzzy majority. *Fuzzy Sets and Systems, 49*(1), 21–31.

Keinan, G. (1987). Decision making under stress: Scanning of alternatives under controllable and uncontrollable threats. *Journal of Personality and Social Psychology, 52*(3), 639–644.

Knighton, R. J. (2004). The psychology of risk and its role in military decision-making. *Defense Studies, 4*(3), 309–334.

Kocet, M. M., McCauley, J., & Thompson, L. (2009). *Ethical decision-making model for student affairs.* Retrieved from http://ebookbrowse.com/kocet-mccauley-thompson-ethical-decision-making-model-sa-revised-doc-d370114178

Kohlberg, L. (1969). Stage and sequence: The cognitive developmental approach to socialization. In D. A. Goslin (Ed.), *Handbook of socialization theory and research* (pp. 347–480). Skokie, IL: Rand McNally.

Levy, S. R., & Kozoll, C. E. (1998). *A guide to decision making in student affairs: A case study approach.* Springfield, IL: Charles C. Thomas.

Lonergan, B. (1973). *Method in theology.* Toronto, Canada: University of Toronto Press.

March, J. G., & Simon, H. A. (1958). *Organizations.* New York, NY: Wiley.

Mazzolini, R. (1981). How strategic decisions are made. *Long Range Planning, 14,* 85–96.

McCown, N. R. (2010). *Developing intuitive decision-making in modern military leadership.* [Paper submitted to the faculty of the Naval War College.] Retrieved from http://www.au.af.mil/au/awc/awcgate/navy/nwc_mccown.pdf

Mintzberg, H., Raisinghani, P., & Theoret, A. (1976). The structure of "unstructured" decision processes. *Administrative Science Quarterly, 21*(2), 246–275.

Mitchell, J. M., & Yordy, E. D. (2010). Cover it: A comprehensive framework for guiding students through ethical dilemmas. *Journal of Legal Studies Education, 27*(1), 35–60.

Nash, R. J. (2002). *"Real world" ethics: Frameworks for educators and human service professionals* (2nd ed.). New York, NY: Teachers College Press.

Park, G., & DeShon, R. P. (2010). A multilevel model of minority opinion expression and team decision-making effectiveness. *Journal of Applied Psychology, 95*(5), 824–833.

Posner, R. A. (1988). The jurisprudence of skepticism. *Michigan Law Review, 86*(5), 827–891.

Rest, J. R. (1986). *Moral development: Advances in research and theory.* New York, NY: Praeger.

Roberts, M. S., & Sonnenberg, F. A. (2000). Decision modeling techniques. In G. B. Chapman & F. A. Sonnenberg (Eds.), *Decision making in health care: Theory, psychology and applications* (pp. 30–64). Cambridge, England: Cambridge University Press.

Roets, A., & Van Hiel, A. (2011). An integrative process approach on judgment and decision making: The impact of arousal, affect, motivation, and cognitive ability. *Psychological Record, 61*(3), 497–520.

Rogerson, M. D., Gottlieb, M. C., Handelsman, M. M., Knapp, S., & Younggren, J. (2011). Nonrational processes in ethical decision making. *American Psychologist, 66*(7), 614–623.

Schwenk, C. R. (1984). Cognitive simplification processes in strategic decision-making. *Strategic Management Journal, 5*(2), 111–128.

Simon, D. (2004). A third view of the black box: Cognitive coherence in legal decision making. *University of Chicago Law Review, 71*, 511–586.

Simon, H. (1982). *Models of bounded rationality and other topics in economics.* Cambridge, MA: MIT Press.

Sonnenberg, F. A., & Beck, J. R. (2008). Markov models in medical decision making: A practical guide. *Medical Decision Making, 13*(4), 322–338.

Terwel, B. W., Harinck, F., Ellemers, N., & Daamen, D. D. L. (2010). Voice in political decision-making: The effect of group voice on perceived trustworthiness of decision makers and subsequent acceptance of decisions. *Journal of Experimental Psychology: Applied, 16*(2), 173–186.

U.S. Department of the Army. (2010). *The operations process* (field manual 5-0). Retrieved from http://www.fas.org/irp/doddir/army/fm5-0.pdf

Weick, K. E. (1995). *Sensemaking in organizations.* Thousand Oaks, CA; Sage.

Zeleny, M. (1982). *Multiple criteria decision making.* New York, NY: McGraw-Hill.

CHAPTER 2

Decision-Making Framework

IN THIS CHAPTER, we share a decision-making framework (DMF) specifically designed for novice student affairs professionals. The DMF is the result of a year-long process of development, vetting, and revisions. The literature described in chapter 1 provided a basic foundation for the DMF, but while we liked many aspects of the decision-making models in the literature, we wanted more detail and more student affairs context. To that end, we mapped effective decision-making processes. After several iterations, we produced a final copy of a decision-making framework that we believed would be a useful resource for graduate students and entry-level student affairs professionals. To determine whether graduate students, new professionals, and their supervisors would find it useful, we piloted the framework with a variety of student affairs audiences.

The first test of the DMF occurred at a NASPA–Student Affairs Administrators in Higher Education conference, where student affairs professionals with various levels of experience applied the framework to sample case studies. In that session, practitioners offered both affirmations of the model and suggestions for improvement. After making some revisions, we piloted the DMF again at three universities, where graduate students were invited to use the framework to work through a sample case study. We used student feedback to revise the DMF again and conducted a third pilot with another set of graduate students. Most of the students were of the millennial generation. They appreciated the level of detail offered in the DMF and the fact that much of the framework was in the form of questions instead of narrowly prescriptive solutions. During the pilot testing, students noted that the questions made them think about issues they would not have otherwise considered.

The DMF questions prompted students to think more deeply about the issues and their responses. This was our goal. Simply telling young professionals how to solve problems is neither educational nor effective. As educators, we wanted to provide a framework that new professionals could use to make effective decisions related to a host of problems, issues, and dilemmas. The DMF requires graduate students and new professionals to consider a variety of issues when responding to a major crisis or minor event. Regardless of the situation, the best response is always one that involves thoughtful reflection and appropriate action. We believe the DMF encourages readers to reflect and act.

Decision-Making Framework Overview

The decision-making framework comprises three components: (1) decision-making phases, (2) tasks, and (3) key questions and considerations. Each of these components is described briefly in the bullets below and more comprehensively in the pages that follow. In the next section, we bring these three components together with context, the other essential element of the DMF, and provide a complete visual overview of the framework. See Figure 2.6 and the color insert.

- **Phases.** The DMF consists of four decision-making phases: (1) identification of the problem, (2) comprehensive scan of the options, (3) implementation, and (4) assessment. These phases describe the process (sequential steps) professionals go through to make effective decisions in difficult situations. As you progress through the case studies in this book, you will use Phases 1–3. You will not be able to implement your decisions in the case studies, so there is no way to assess your success. However, we hope you will make use of Phase 4 in real-life situations. Figure 2.1 is a visual representation of the four phases. Each phase is associated with an icon: pentagon, square, triangle, circle. These icons are used throughout the book.
- **Tasks.** Each decision-making phase includes a series of tasks. While the decision-making phases are broad, the tasks are specific.
- **Key Questions and Considerations.** One of the unique aspects of the DMF is the use of key questions and considerations. We believe it is important to offer new professionals a sequential guide of decision-making phases and tasks, but we also wanted to ensure that they thoughtfully reflect on the complexity of problem situations. Thus, each decision-making phase and each task is accompanied by a series of questions.

Figure 2.1

The Four Phases of the Decision-Making Framework

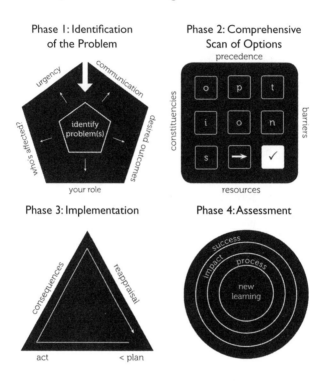

Phase 1: Identification of the Problem

Phase 2: Comprehensive Scan of Options

Phase 3: Implementation

Phase 4: Assessment

In the following pages, we describe each phase of the DMF in detail and explain how higher education professionals can use the framework. Each decision-making phase is accompanied by tasks that novice professionals should accomplish before proceeding to the next phase. We also summarize the salient questions that should be answered to accomplish each task.

Phase 1: Identification of the Problem

Too often, professionals leap to problem solving without conducting a thorough assessment of the problems or issues. Three key tasks guide professionals through the process of identifying the core and related problems to be addressed. These tasks are summarized in Figure 2.2.

Figure 2.2

Phase 1: Identification of the Problem

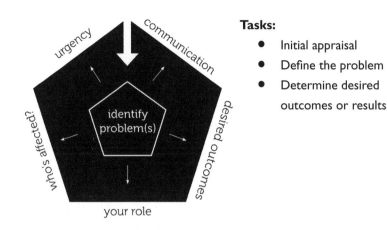

Tasks:
- Initial appraisal
- Define the problem
- Determine desired outcomes or results

The first task is to conduct an initial appraisal of the core problem. Issues of urgency, threat assessment, and victim vulnerability are a priority at the beginning of Phase 1. Life-threatening situations in which someone is in immediate danger—such as a shooter on campus—immediately come to mind. However, more subtle issues of threat might be overlooked or underestimated; for example, when a residence hall door has been left open for 4 hours during the night or a tornado warning is not seriously considered.

Complex and simple problems often necessitate a combination of immediate and long-term solutions. One of the considerations in the initial appraisal is to determine how urgent the problem is. If two students are about to start a brawl in the dining hall, you are dealing with an immediate situation. As part of this task, you also need to assess the level of threat, if any, that a situation poses to students, staff, faculty, and the community. In some cases, you might need to determine what effects an incident has already had on key stakeholders. Finally, during the initial appraisal (and throughout the decision-making process), you should consider whom (e.g., supervisors, colleagues, campus police) you need to inform or consult. No professional is an island, and no incident or crisis should ever involve just you.

- **Task:** Initial appraisal.
- **Key questions and considerations:**
  ◊ What is the core problem to be addressed?
  ◊ What is the urgency of this problem?
  ◊ What is the level of threat for individuals or the campus community?
  ◊ What persons or groups (e.g., faculty, students, staff) are being or have been most affected by this problem?
  ◊ What immediate actions must be taken to handle any crisis aspects of this problem?
  ◊ Whom do you need to inform/consult as you move forward?

Once the initial appraisal is complete, you are encouraged to more accurately define the problem, which is the second task associated with Phase 1. During the initial appraisal, professionals often do not have all the pertinent facts because things are happening quickly. This is especially true in crisis situations, when professionals are pressed to make sense of a situation in a hurry. As the case of General Mattis reminds us (McCown, 2010), immediate judgment and action are often necessary; however, most problems cannot be fully understood in an instant. Obtaining more information is important to effectively define complex problems. Collecting data can include reading documents (i.e., reports, e-mail), listening to people's stories, or witnessing an event firsthand. Once you have collected the available facts, you might find that you have a new or different understanding of the problem. Or you might uncover secondary or residual problems associated with your initial concern. For example, in the situation in which a residence hall door was left open for 4 hours, you might have to consider that an intruder could be hiding in the facility or might have unlocked a window to create future access to the residence hall.

As situations develop, you can gain a more comprehensive understanding of the problem. Sometimes this is done through solitary reflection; often, however, understanding of complex issues results from consultation with other professionals, including supervisors, peers, and experts (e.g., counselors, public safety officers). Thus, an essential element of this task is to find out what the parties involved see as the problem and how they are handling it. Perhaps the student who left the door open in the residence hall views it as a minor lapse in judgment, while other students in the hall see it as a major threat to their safety.

As you continue to define the problem, you need to clarify your role in the situation and the roles of all parties involved. In some situations, your role might be to respond to a student immediately. In other cases—such as one in which a student might have a weapon—your role would be to contact campus police for an intervention. You might also have been instructed about safety protocols such as lockdowns, in which your role is more expansive.

- **Task:** Define the problem.
- **Key questions and considerations:**
  - ◊ What do the parties involved see as the problem? How are they handling their involvement in the problem?
  - ◊ What is your role in this situation? How much authority/responsibility do you have?
  - ◊ What information is needed to develop a clear understanding of the problem?
  - ◊ How will you gather the information you need to define the problem?
  - ◊ After considering all the available facts, do you have a new or different understanding of the initial problem?
  - ◊ What other issues or problems are associated with the core problem?

A final task in Phase 1 is to determine desired outcomes. Determining appropriate interventions is impossible unless you know what ideal (or less than ideal) results might look like. You cannot move forward with effective decision making unless you have thought about what you hope to accomplish in the short term and long term. As noted earlier, solutions to complex problems often involve ongoing responses—you might have to engage in both immediate and subsequent problem solving. For your actions to be most effective, you need to consider both short- and long-term solutions. A short-term solution to an impending hurricane or tornado would likely be to move students to a safe place. Long-term solutions could involve property recovery and rearranging classrooms, offices, or student living arrangements while damaged buildings are repaired. A final element of this task is to think about the impact the outcomes might have on the campus community. Thinking about your desires for the short and long run will help you complete a truly comprehensive scan of the options, which is Phase 2.

- **Task:** Determine desired outcomes or results.
- **Key questions and considerations:**
   ◊ What do you hope will happen in the short run to alleviate any immediate stress caused by the problem?
   ◊ What do you hope will happen in the long run (outcomes) as a result of any actions you might take?
   ◊ What impact will these outcomes have on the campus community?

Phase 2: Comprehensive Scan of Options

Complex problems often cannot be resolved with simple solutions. Instead, student affairs professionals must grapple with a variety of possible responses to a problem or issue to determine which solution(s) might be most effective. This phase includes two tasks, which are summarized in Figure 2.3

Figure 2.3

Phase 2: Comprehensive Scan of Options

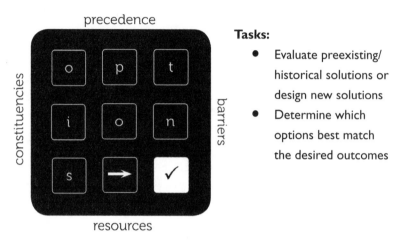

Tasks:

- Evaluate preexisting/ historical solutions or design new solutions
- Determine which options best match the desired outcomes

Your first task in Phase 2 is to evaluate preexisting or historical solutions. For instance, you should learn how similar situations have been handled in the past, either at your school or at peer institutions. In ideal situations, graduate students and new professionals are trained on policies and protocols for their institution and department. The more information you have about how your institution typically handles situations, the better situated you will be to make effective decisions. If you are not in a department that offers such training, do not wait for an event to happen to learn about policies, protocols, and the way things are done on your campus. Be proactive and use the resources around you to learn as much as you can. Be sure to talk with supervisors and mentors who can help you gain a more thorough understanding of realistic solutions.

- **Task:** Evaluate preexisting/historical solutions or design new solutions.
- **Key questions and considerations:**
  - ◊ How has this type of problem been handled in the past at this institution or at another institution where you have worked?
  - ◊ What protocols/guidelines/resources are available to handle this type of situation?
  - ◊ What ideas are available from staff members, supervisors, or mentors about how to handle this situation?
  - ◊ What specific options are (or are not) available to you at this point?

Once you have considered the possible solutions, your next task is to decide which options best match your desired outcomes. One of the most important aspects of this task is to determine whether barriers (political, fiscal, personnel, etc.) exist to some of your possible options. If so, you will need to decide whether those barriers are surmountable. For instance, an ideal solution might require a significant amount of funding. Or your ideas for a solution might require permission from the university president or state legislature. Or your plans to resolve a situation might require the participation of orientation leaders or student affairs supervisors on campus. Obtaining funding, permissions, or human resources might not be realistic in your situation—your choices must fall within the bounds of your resources. An effective problem solver can identify necessary resources and determine whether those resources are obtainable.

As you consider potential options, you will also need to think about how each solution might adversely affect stakeholders. To determine this, you must be knowledgeable about possible constituents (e.g., students, parents, alumni, faculty, staff, community members) and how they might be affected. When a suicide occurs on campus, for example, some students might be traumatized by the event and need counseling, parents might have concerns that their child is in danger, alumni might be concerned about the campus climate, and staff might be worried about the well-being of other students they work with. In this task, and throughout the decision-making process, it is important for you to be in tune with the needs and concerns of various stakeholders.

Decision making is about reflection and action, but it is also about communication. A solution might affect different constituents in different ways, so it is important to be able to communicate your plans and rationale to a variety of stakeholders. In the case of a suicide, decisions about informing families take priority over all other considerations. Ceremonies or memorial services must be discussed with families and friends before any plans are made. Counseling center personnel, campus ministry, residence life staff, and faculty can all play a role in meeting student needs for healing.

- **Task:** Determine which options best match the desired outcomes.
- **Key questions and considerations:**
  - ◊ For each option, what barriers might prevent you from moving toward the desired outcomes?
  - ◊ Are there any constituents (student groups, parents, alumni, departments, staff, community members) who might be negatively affected by the choice of a particular option, thus impeding the desired outcome?
  - ◊ How will you justify your choice to these constituents?
  - ◊ What resources (e.g., financial, personnel) will you need to implement each option?
  - ◊ After weighing the pros and cons of each option, which one is most likely to move you toward your desired outcomes?

Phase 3: Implementation

Now that you have completed a comprehensive scan of the options, you should be able to effectively communicate your specific plan of action to others. It is also time for implementation. During Phase 3, you will put your plan into action. The two tasks associated with this phase are summarized in Figure 2.4.

Figure 2.4

Phase 3: Implementation

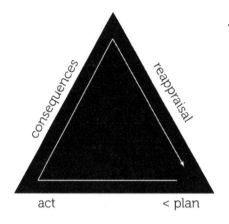

Tasks:

- Move forward with your solution
- Possible reappraisal of your plan of action

As you move forward with your solution, make sure you have thought through all the necessary steps for smooth implementation. Your solution likely involves a variety of activities, such as phone calls, e-mails, reports, individual and group meetings, or interpersonal interventions. Solutions, however, require more than activities; they involve people. It is unlikely that you will be the only person involved in implementation, as professionals rarely solve problems in isolation. Some of the people and agencies who could assist with implementation are your supervisor, colleagues, student employees, student leaders, campus safety, other campus personnel, and community agencies (e.g., police, rape crisis center). You will need to communicate to others the tasks they need to perform and the time frame in which those tasks should be accomplished. In the example of the open door in the residence hall, you might decide that a person from campus safety should check the building immediately. You might also talk with your staff and the resident assistants so they are aware of the situation and prepared to inform residents, if necessary. Without clear communication among all parties, implementation can fail.

- **Task:** Move forward with your solution.
- **Key questions and considerations:**
  ◊ What is your specific plan of action?
  ◊ What tasks must be accomplished to move forward with your plan?
  ◊ Who will perform the necessary tasks?
  ◊ What is your prioritized time frame for each of these tasks?

No matter how well thought out an implementation plan is, unintended consequences can occur. As you move forward, stay abreast of emerging concerns and unanticipated consequences. Effectively addressing emerging issues is just as important as solving the initial problem. Student affairs professionals are constantly reappraising situations and solutions. Through the reappraisal process, you might find that your efforts are not going as planned. If that is the case, you might need to change your strategy. Perhaps, for example, you have implemented a plan to resettle a large group of students who have "occupied" the quad outside your campus center. You have provided an alternative space near one of your residence halls, and most of the occupiers are in the process of moving when you discover that the new site blocks major fire exits and access areas. Finding another site might be one alternative; removing the occupiers entirely is another.

- **Task:** Possible reappraisal of your plan of action.
- **Key questions and considerations:**
  ◊   What is your strategy for dealing with unforeseen issues, unintended consequences, or problems related to the implementation of your plan?
  ◊   Is your initial appraisal of the problem on target, or does the problem need to be reappraised?
  ◊   Are there any changes in your plan or strategy at this point?

If you determine that your decisions and solutions are not going as planned, you might need to return to Phase 1 to reconsider your understanding of the problem. You might have misinterpreted or misunderstood the core problem or the complexity of an issue. We all make mistakes, and even the most seasoned practitioners can misread a situation. Part of making good decisions is the willingness to reflect, admit mistakes, and adapt. If you believe that you have a comprehensive understanding of the problem but your strategy is ineffective, you might need to return to Phase 2 and explore other options.

Phase 4: Assessment

The ongoing awareness and reappraisal associated with Phase 3 should not replace a final assessment of outcomes, which is Phase 4 in the DMF. Assessment is a critical component of the profession of student affairs. In our field, we understand the importance of learning from both our successes and mistakes. The assessment phase contains two tasks, summarized in Figure 2.5.

Figure 2.5

Phase 4: Assessment

Tasks:

- Reflect on the impact and success of your solutions
- Reflect on your implementation process and new learning

Once you have implemented your solutions, you are not finished. After implementation, you should reflect on the success and impact of your actions, and whether you achieved the outcomes you set in Phase 1. Also, you might need to address unanticipated outcomes at this point. Consult a variety of constituents to determine how successful they think your implementation was—you might think it went well, but your colleagues or supervisor might feel differently.

- **Task:** Reflect on the impact and success of your solutions.
- **Key questions and considerations:**
  - ◊ Were the desired outcomes achieved?
  - ◊ Do any unanticipated outcomes need to be addressed?
  - ◊ With whom did you consult to determine the impact of your plan/solution?

Beyond solutions and impact, you should also consider your decision-making process. Effective problem solvers learn from their successes and mistakes in both outcomes and processes. At this point in the DMF, an important task is to reflect on what you learned from the situation and your decision-making process. Hindsight often provides new ways of thinking about decision-making style, communication patterns, and leadership skills. Candid self-assessment of your skills and shortcomings can help you more effectively manage future problems and crises. As part of this task, you also have an opportunity to assess the effectiveness of policies, programs, and protocols (or lack thereof) at your institution. As you made decisions, did you find policies, programs, or protocols adequate for the situation? Do they need to be modified to more effectively address similar incidents in the future?

- **Task:** Reflect on your implementation process and new learning.
- **Key questions and considerations:**
    - ◊   What can you learn from your mistakes and successes?
    - ◊   What might you do differently next time?
    - ◊   What did you learn about your decision-making style? How might this new knowledge help you in the future?
    - ◊   What policies, programs, or protocols need to be reviewed or put into place to prevent similar situations from occurring in the future?

The Decision-Making Framework in Context

Now that you have been introduced to the DMF's phases, tasks, and key questions and considerations, you are ready to think more broadly about the framework. Figure 2.6 and the color insert show how the developmental framework flows from an initial event to identification of the problem, scan of options, implementation, and assessment. In many situations, you can follow the arrow through these stages. However, if you encounter lack of success or unanticipated consequences, you may need to return to Phase 1 or Phase 2 to revisit the problem or the possible options.

Figure 2.6

Decision-Making Framework Flow Diagram

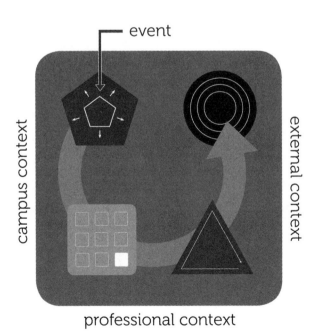

No problem exists in a vacuum and neither should your solutions. Every incident, crisis, and event happens at an historical point in time. No two moments in history are precisely the same nor are the institutional contexts in which they occur. Figure 2.6 illustrates the significance of context. You will notice that three specific contexts surround the image of the DMF: (1) professional, (2) campus, and (3) external.

Professional Context

The context of the student affairs profession informs our daily practice. Professional context can include historical documents, ethical standards, developmental theories, and contemporary research in the field. Some historical guideposts in student affairs are documents such as *The Student Personnel Point of View* (American Council on Education, 1937, 1949); *The Student Learning Imperative: Implications for Student Affairs* (American College Personnel Association [ACPA], 1994); *Standards of Professional Practice* (NASPA, 1990); and *Principles of Good Practice for Student Affairs* (ACPA & NASPA, 1996). Professional context is also informed by statements of ethical principles (e.g., ACPA, 2006). In fact, this book was inspired by *Professional Competency Areas for Student Affairs Practitioners* (ACPA & NASPA, 2010). These competencies—along with ethical standards of our profession, student development theory, and cutting-edge research—should guide your decision-making processes, no matter how large or small the decisions.

Campus Context

The second context to consider is your campus. Institution type, size, culture, and climate should inform your decision-making process. There are more than 4,600 degree-granting institutions of higher education in the United States (U.S. Department of Education National Center for Education Statistics, 2011), offering a wide variety of learning environments. Often we group institutions into categories to help us understand their different natures. For instance, colleges and universities are classified by an emphasis on the degrees offered, such as associate, bachelor's, master's, or doctoral. Institutions of higher education are also often categorized by the primary funding sources (e.g., public, private, for profit). Additionally, institutions can be classified by other dimensions, such as size, affiliation, selectivity, residential living, academic focus, curricular focus, and student population. Beyond these classification criteria, colleges and universities vary greatly in their missions, cultures, and political realities.

In *Where You Work Matters*, Hirt (2006) explained how student affairs work is shaped by the unique histories, missions, environments, relationships, and rewards at a variety of postsecondary institutions (e.g., liberal arts, religiously affiliated, comprehensive, research, community colleges, historically Black colleges and universities [HBCUs], and Hispanic-serving institutions [HSIs]). We believe that campus context also matters in decision making. While your decision-making process should always follow the four DMF phases, it will be shaped by the institutional context. For instance, the context for decision making may vary among a liberal arts institution, a community college, and an HBCU. An event that is viewed as problematic at one type of school might not be a problem at another. A similar incident might require very different interventions at a small religiously affiliated institution and a large public institution. Student affairs professionals at religiously affiliated institutions might need to ask themselves, "What is the stance of the religious founders of this institution?"

Institution size can also influence how decisions are made and communicated. Smaller institutions may have fewer levels of administration and authority, fewer physical resources, and smaller numbers of support personnel. On the other hand, information might travel more quickly to students and staff at small institutions than at larger ones. Thus, while large institutions may have sufficient campus facilities to manage an outbreak of the newest strain of a highly contagious flu, smaller institutions may have to rely on local health care facilities. However, directives can be communicated and containment more easily accomplished on a small campus.

Every higher education institution has a unique culture. Tierney (1990) described culture as "deeply embedded patterns of organizational behavior and the shared values, assumptions and beliefs, or ideologies that members have about their organization or their work" (p. 6). Kuh and Whitt (1988) referred to culture as "the social and normative glue . . . that holds organizations together" (p. 10). For example, the culture at a Jesuit institution might value service to humanity through Catholicism. In this context, Jesuit values, traditions, and rituals could influence your entire decision-making process, from your understanding of the initial problem to realistic options, methods of implementation, and assessment.

Cultural values, ideologies, rituals, and norms might be easier to identify at some institutions than at others, but every institution has a culture. The key questions and considerations in Phase 1 include "What is your role in this situation?" and "How much authority and responsibility do you have?" Similarly, in Phase 2, you are asked to consider "How has this type of problem been handled in the past at your institution?" If you know the institutional context, you can effectively answer these questions and respond in a manner that aligns with your campus culture. If you work at a campus where the cultural norm is for senior professionals to implement all solutions to campus crises, your decision-making process should reflect this reality. Conversely, if you work in a campus culture where senior administrators take a hands-off approach to problems, you might have the authority and autonomy to make very different decisions. In short, you must know your own campus culture to find solutions that will work.

While campus culture is an enduring sense of deeply shared beliefs, norms, and values, climate is less enduring and widespread. Climate typically refers to current perceptions or attitudes about an organization. It is "the current common patterns of important dimensions of organizational life or its members' perceptions of and attitudes toward those dimensions . . . [and is] concerned with current perceptions and attitudes rather than deeply held meanings, beliefs, and values" (Tierney, 1990, p. 7). Your solutions to a racial incident on a campus that has had a number of race riots might be very different from your decisions at an institution where intergroup race relations among students, staff, and faculty are frequent and overwhelmingly positive.

External Context

The third context for decision making is the external community. External context can include the political and cultural context of the town, state, or region where your campus is located. If you work in a small community where local politicians regularly exert influence on campus affairs, your decision making might look different than if you work at a school that has very little relationship with the local community.

No matter where you work, local events (celebrations, tragedies, etc.) can influence your decision making. Imagine that you work at a school in a town where a series of highly publicized rapes has been reported. Or imagine that your school is in a city that has recently passed a number of anti-immigration bills. Sociopolitical contexts such as these can shape not only your decision-making options but also how well your solutions are received by the external community. Consider the earlier example of the open door in the residence hall. Did you think that an open door was not very important and would not require reflective or strategic decision making? Imagine that it is an all-women's residence hall and your college is located in a town that has had a string of highly publicized and violent rapes. The perpetrator has not been apprehended. How might this external context inform your decision-making process?

National and global contexts also serve as external backdrops for your work as a professional. For instance, the options available for solving problems may be limited during fiscal crises or more abundant in stable economic times. If you determine that a long-term solution to a campus problem is to offer more diversity training for student and professional staff, then you might be able to afford to hire social justice consultants during good economic times. However, during a recession, those trainings may need to be facilitated by campus experts who can be rewarded with appreciation and praise.

Summary

In this chapter, we presented the elements of the DMF: the four developmental phases, the tasks, and the key questions and considerations. We believe that it is also essential to reflect on professional, campus, and external contexts in the decision-making process. While no model is perfect, the DMF is offered as a guide for decision making. Because decision making is not a totally linear process, we encourage you to adapt the process to arrive at the most successful outcome.

As you move through the remainder of the book, we suggest that you revisit this chapter often. One reading is not enough to memorize the details of the framework. We have included a color insert with a summary of the DMF for your use as you navigate the case studies. You can also use the insert when you encounter real-life situations.

It is our hope that as you grow as a professional, you will come to rely less on the insert and develop your own natural and intuitive decision-making process. As you use the DMF and gain real-life decision-making experience, you will find that your gut reactions to problems are shaped by the DMF. You will begin to intuitively navigate through real-world problems by asking yourself key questions to determine the nature of the problem, scanning your options, implementing solutions, and assessing your success. Like General Mattis, you will develop an intuitive sense of how to solve problems. Our intent is for you to use the DMF as a training tool to help you develop your own personalized response to dilemmas.

REFERENCES

American College Personnel Association (ACPA). (1994). *The student learning imperative: Implications for student affairs.* Washington, DC: Author.

American College Personnel Association (ACPA). (2006). *Statement of ethical principles and standards.* Retrieved from http://www.myacpa.org/au/documents/Ethical_Principles_Standards.pdf

American College Personnel Association (ACPA) and National Association of Student Personnel Administrators (NASPA). (1996). *Principles of good practice for student affairs.* Retrieved from http://www.naspa.org/career/goodprac.cfm

American College Personnel Association (ACPA) and National Association of Student Personnel Administrators (NASPA). (2010). *Professional competency areas for student affairs practitioners.* Retrieved from http://www.naspa.org/programs/prodev/Professional_Competencies.pdf

American Council on Education. (1937). *The student personnel point of view.* Washington, DC: Author.

American Council on Education. (1949). *The student personnel point of view.* Washington, DC: Author.

Hirt, J. B. (2006). *Where you work matters: Student affairs administration at different types of institutions.* Lanham, MD: University Press.

Kuh, G. D., & Whitt, E. J. (1988). *The invisible tapestry: Culture in American colleges and universities.* Washington, DC: Association for the Study of Higher Education.

McCown, N. R. (2010). *Developing intuitive decision-making in modern military leadership*. [Paper submitted to the faculty of the Naval War College.] Retrieved from http://www.au.af.mil/au/awc/awcgate/navy/nwc_mccown.pdf

National Association of Student Personnel Administrators (NASPA). (1990). *Standards of professional practice*. Retrieved from http://www.naspa.org/about/standards.cfm

Tierney, W. G. (Ed.). (1990). *Assessing academic climates and cultures* (New directions for institutional research, No. 68). San Francisco, CA: Jossey-Bass.

U.S. Department of Education National Center for Education Statistics. (2011). *Fast facts*. Retrieved from http://nces.ed.gov/fastfacts/display.asp?id=84

CHAPTER 3

Sample Case Study

IN THIS CHAPTER, we provide a sample case study analysis to show how the decision-making framework (DMF) can be used to identify a problem, scan the options, implement solutions, and assess outcomes and process. We encourage you to read through this sample case before you tackle the cases in chapter 4.

The sample case study, called "To Tweet or Not to Tweet," is based on an incident that actually occurred on a college campus. The institution, names, and a few facts were changed in the interest of confidentiality. In preparation for writing this chapter, the four authors simulated a classroom activity in which we read the sample case and applied the DMF. In the simulation, we discussed how we would like to see Chandra, the student affairs professional who is the focus of the event, progress through the DMF. This chapter summarizes the highlights of the conversation and reflects the way we, as four professionals representing very different worldviews, worked through DMF Phases 1–3. It is impossible for us to know the outcomes of the fictional decisions we are making for Chandra. Yet, assessment is an essential aspect of the decision-making process. Therefore, we selected a sample case that reflects an actual event in order to demonstrate how Phase 4 of the DMF was used in real-life. We conclude the chapter with a summary of the ways each of the 10 competency areas can be related to the decision-making process and outcomes.

To Tweet or Not to Tweet

Chandra is the assistant director of student activities at St. Andrews College, a small, private, Roman Catholic liberal arts college in a rural community. The student population is approximately 1,800; 85% of the students live on campus.

As assistant director of student activities, Chandra oversees many of the college's clubs and organizations, and she provides support to the director of student activities, Lynn Ellis. The director works closely with the Student Government Association (SGA) and its executive board. Chandra and Lynn co-advise the SGA. Lynn reports to the dean of students, Bill Gauge. The campus has a very casual work climate in which the chain of command is not always followed to address an issue. It is not unusual for the dean of students or a director to call Chandra directly to discuss a situation.

Recently, Father Champlin, the president of St. Andrews, opened a Twitter account to connect with students and alumni. He is still learning the ropes, but many students are following him, and he has elected to follow them as well.

This week, Chandra is alone in the office. Lynn is away on her honeymoon and has asked Chandra not to contact her unless it is an emergency. It is Monday morning and Chandra receives a phone call from the president's office requesting that she meet with Fr. Champlin. She immediately goes to his office. He tells her that over the weekend he was reading the tweets of the SGA president, Jake Jacobs, and was appalled at the level of profanity. Furthermore, Jake was using the SGA Twitter account, not a personal account, to criticize the college—specifically, public safety and residence life—for breaking up parties and not allowing students to drink alcohol on campus. Fr. Champlin asks Chandra to address this issue with Jake and have him stop the negative tweets about St. Andrews immediately, even if it means shutting down the Twitter account.

APPLYING THE DECISION-MAKING FRAMEWORK

In the following pages, we use the DMF to analyze this case. Before applying the key questions and considerations, we discuss the professional, campus, and external contexts, which are paramount and should shape every aspect of decision making, from understanding the problem to scanning possible options, implementing solutions, and assessing outcomes.

Professional Context

The relevant professional context for this case includes ethical principles and standards of the profession of student affairs. These guidelines could shape the way Chandra makes meaning of the situation and how her decision-making process evolves. In our processing of the case, we considered ethical issues related to Jake's use of a college account to disparage St. Andrews.

Another possible professional context is the growing use of social media in student affairs. Social media are a contemporary reality, and student affairs practitioners must possess knowledge of the law as it relates to these media (Hutchens, 2012). Professionals must also have basic technological skills to address incidents such as this one. Technology is not one of the 10 professional competency areas for student affairs practitioners. Rather, it is described as a "thread" that functions as an "essential element" in all the competency areas (ACPA & NASPA, 2010, p. 5). The contemporary professional context of social media, then, is one in which practitioners are expected to understand and appropriately manage technology in their daily work. Technological understanding and skills are certainly important in this case study.

Campus Context

The second element for this case is the campus context—a number of institutional realities could inform the decision-making process. St. Andrews is a small, private, religious college, so the Catholic Church's perspective must be considered. The culture of an institution steeped in religious teachings, coupled with the casual climate of the student affairs division, might inform how Chandra understands the problem, reviews potential options, and proceeds with implementation. Chandra also might need to think about the limitations on student rights at private colleges compared with public schools. The fact that the college president is a novice Twitter user also shapes this case. Finally, the history of public safety interactions with students (e.g., historically hostile or friendly) and the party/drinking culture on campus might provide contextual backdrops for decision making in this case.

External Context

The third context is an external one. St. Andrews is not an island; it exists in the context of a twenty-first-century political, social, and economic environment. The influence of technology extends from larger societal realities. Technology is ever more important in how people communicate. Thus, it is not merely a thread in the student affairs professional competencies; it is also a global reality.

St. Andrews, as a religiously affiliated institution, is situated in the larger sociopolitical context of the Catholic Church. Political realities, such as religious scandals, might not seem relevant to the case at St. Andrews, but college administrators may be sensitive to *any* bad press. Another aspect of the external context includes other constituencies that have (or could have) a relationship with St. Andrews. Negative tweets and the college response to the tweets might affect the way prospective students, alumni, donors, and local community members view St. Andrews. Mismanagement of this situation could beget bad press, which could, in turn, have long-term political or economic ramifications for St. Andrews.

DEVELOPMENTAL PHASES

As the four authors worked through the case study, the professional, campus, and external contexts were at the forefront. These contexts informed our discussion as we moved into the three developmental phases of the DMF. In the following pages, we describe how we thought Chandra should proceed through Phases 1–3 of the DMF. After our analysis of Phases 1–3, we summarize Chandra's actual response to the case and her real-life assessment (Phase 4) of the situation.

Phase 1: Identification of the Problem

Task: Initial appraisal

What is the core problem to be addressed? In contemporary student affairs situations such as the one described in this case, a professional's first job is to make an initial appraisal of the core problem or problems. There are a variety of possibilities in this case. The core problem could be Jake's tweets and the impact they have on the campus and local community. Another problem could be that Jake engaged in inappropriate behavior as a student leader by using a college Twitter account to criticize the school. Some people might see the core problem as a conflict between the values of the institution and a student's freedom of expression. Is the president stifling a student's right to voice his opinion, or is he acting appropriately to protect the reputation of the college? Or could it be both? Another perspective might focus on the fact that a college president was following students on Twitter: Some people might view informal social media interactions between a president and students as a recipe for disaster, while others might see such relations as a positive reflection of community. Or the problem could be connected to the fact that a student leader was affirming a culture of underage binge drinking. Or is the issue an overly aggressive public safety office?

The four authors discussed each of these possibilities at length. Initially, each of us saw the core problem in a slightly different light. However, in the case study, as in real-life situations, a decision must be made about the core problem(s) before a practitioner can progress through the DMF. That is not to say that the problem cannot be reassessed; indeed, a later question in Phase 1 asks, "After considering all the available facts, do you have a new or different understanding of the initial problem?" Again in Phase 3, the DMF asks whether the initial appraisal of the core problem is on target or if it needs to be reappraised. So that we could move forward with our simulation of the case study, the four authors agreed that we would define the core problems as follows: Chandra is an entry-level professional who has been directed by the president to deal with inappropriate language and harsh criticism of the school by a student leader. Part of the problem is that the student used a college Twitter account to air his complaints.

What is the urgency of this problem? What is the level of threat for individuals or the campus community? In our discussion about the urgency of the problem and the threat level, we considered a variety of perspectives. At first glance there seemed to be no physical threat or safety issues that would heighten the urgency of the problem. However, the Internet is a fluid entity. Jake's critical comments could spread virally, which could potentially incite nonvirtual and disruptive campus behavior such as protests and vandalism.

We also considered Chandra's role in the college. As an entry-level student affairs professional who was called by the president, she would understandably perceive the problem as urgent. We decided that while the problem per se might not be urgent, it was politically important and should be Chandra's top priority at least for the day.

What persons or groups (e.g., faculty, students, staff) are being or have been most affected by this problem? Obviously, the president has been affected by the tweets. Because he called Chandra, the problem will now affect her, as well as her supervisor and the dean of students. Everything professionals do affects their supervisors in some way.

Even though Lynn is away from campus, the tweets and the decisions regarding this incident will sooner or later end up on her desk.

Given the electronic nature of Jake's complaints, the impact of the problem might be difficult to assess immediately. Because some of the negative tweets were about the residence halls, the residence life staff could be affected, especially if the incident occurred at the time of the year when students decide whether to live on campus or seek off-campus housing. Anyone using Twitter, and the people with whom they communicate, could be influenced to live off campus. Parents of prospective students who have seen or heard about the tweets might not want their child to live on campus or attend the college at all. Since the tweets could influence prospective students, the admissions office could also be affected.

The alumni relations office might be concerned about negative press influencing alumni and other potential donors. Because the situation involves the use of a college account, information technology staff might also be affected as the situation progresses. Finally, Jake is a leader in the SGA. While individual SGA members may not have been immediately affected by his tweets, they may be touched by the college response.

What immediate actions must be taken to handle any crisis aspects of this problem? The four authors did not view the situation as an immediate crisis, like a fire, tornado, or shooter on campus. In such crisis situations, safety protocols and emergency plans would ideally be in place. In this case, we believe that Chandra's immediate actions might include reviewing all the tweets to see what was actually said. Then she might discuss the problem and possible solutions with the dean of students. She might also locate Jake to request a meeting.

Whom do you need to inform/consult as you move forward? Even though Lynn is out of town, Chandra should at least leave a message informing her of the situation and her tentative plans. Lynn did not want to be contacted unless it was an emergency, but the president's involvement seems to make this incident important enough to warrant getting in touch with her. It is crucial for entry-level professionals to communicate with their superiors, even if they believe the supervisors already have ample information. The next professional staff member in the hierarchy is the dean of students. Chandra should pass her ideas by him and keep him abreast of the situation. Finally, young professionals often reach out to trusted mentors when they need guidance in complicated situations. Chandra might want to call a mentor to discuss her ideas, especially as her direct supervisor is out of town.

Task: Define the problem

What do the parties involved see as the problem? How are they handling their involvement in the problem? Initially, Chandra is privy to the feelings of only one party: the president. She knows he is concerned about the level of profanity and the amount of criticism in the tweets, which he fears could damage the school's reputation. He has decided to become involved in the situation by telling Chandra to deal with the problem immediately.

Until Chandra has a conversation with Jake, she cannot know how he views the situation. The content of his tweets suggests how he feels about partying, but it is impossible to assess his views on the impact of his tweets. Jake may see the situation and his behavior (i.e., using a university account as a vehicle for criticism) as nonproblematic. He may believe that he has the right (and duty) as SGA president to air his opinions. He may be planning to tweet more negative comments soon. On the other hand, Jake may not have considered how his behavior could be problematic. Once this perspective is brought to his attention, he may feel remorseful and be interested in minimizing the damage.

What is your role in this situation? In Lynn's absence, Chandra's role is to handle the situation as directed by the president. If the dean of students instructed Chandra to defer the handling of this situation to him, she would play whatever role the dean asked her to play (e.g., support, back-up, none). As co-advisor to the SGA, she oversees their behavior. One of her duties as a student affairs educator is to have educational conversations with all involved parties, including Jake and the other SGA members.

How much authority/responsibility do you have? As a St. Andrew's employee, Chandra must make an effort to respond to the president's request. She may not have much power to stop or sanction Jake, but she is responsible for trying to manage the situation. As SGA co-advisor, she certainly has some authority and the right to request a meeting with Jake. As we considered Chandra's level of authority, we came to the conclusion that it is unlikely that she has the power to stop or remove Twitter communications, and she certainly cannot control how frequently Jake's comments are re-tweeted from other accounts.

What information is needed to develop a clear understanding of the problem? Many pieces of information are needed to understand the problem. First, if she has not already done so, it would be important for Chandra to review the actual tweets so she has an accurate understanding of the content. Second, she should collect information on any relevant campus protocols, policies, or precedents at St. Andrews if she is not already familiar with them. Finally, she can glean valuable information and perspectives from the parties involved (e.g., information technology, residence life).

How will you gather the information you need to define the problem? To read the tweets, Chandra will visit the SGA Twitter account. She may need to review college publications and view college websites to learn about protocols and policies. Precedent can sometimes be difficult to assess, because such information is often passed on informally by word of mouth. However, Chandra may find hints of precedent in incident reports, annual reports, or other office files. Finally, Chandra will need to engage in direct communications (phone, e-mail) with the parties involved.

After considering all the available facts, do you have a new or different understanding of the initial problem? In a case study (as opposed to a real-life situation), it is difficult to determine whether the understanding of the initial problem has changed. While we can speculate, case study simulations do not allow us to actually collect information that might lead us to view the initial problem differently. In real life, student affairs professionals might gain a different understanding of a problem once they have communicated with the parties involved. For instance, in conversations with Jake, Chandra may learn that he was not the one who posted the tweets; rather, it was a fellow SGA member who thought it would be funny to impersonate Jake.

What other issues or problems are associated with the core problem? One of the possible issues associated with the core problem is that other St. Andrews students might be influenced by Jake's tweets and also criticize the college via social media. And as we mentioned earlier, critical tweets might cause additional problems (e.g., lowered enrollment, reduced donations) with prospective students, alumni, and other external constituents. A related problem might be the issue of freedom of speech at a religious institution. How will Jake and his peers respond to institutional suggestions that they stop or censor their tweets? Depending on the data she collects, Chandra may find that related issues include an overzealous public safety office or a student culture that values partying and drinking. Finally, a related problem might be that Chandra is an entry-level professional who has been asked to make relatively high-level decisions in the absence of her supervisor.

Task: Determine desired outcomes or results

What do you hope will happen in the short run to alleviate any immediate stress caused by the problem? In the short run, we hope Chandra would locate and have a conversation with Jake. Ideally, Jake will understand his responsibility to use the college Twitter account in a fashion that appropriately reflects his role as a student leader. We would also like Jake to understand how his tweets might contribute to a culture of underage drinking—a culture that has legal and health implications. In this scenario, Jake will immediately cease his profanity-laden criticism of the college. We also hope that the president feels satisfied with Chandra's actions.

What do you hope will happen in the long run (outcomes) as a result of any actions you might take? While we hope that Jake immediately stops his foul-mouthed tweets, our long-term expectations go beyond behavior change. Ideally, we hope Jake learns about the responsibility vested in the role of SGA president. The developmental foundation of the student affairs profession undergirds our hope that Chandra's conversation and subsequent interactions with Jake will be educational. Long-term outcomes would include Jake's engaging in more responsible use of social media.

If, in Chandra's search for policies, procedures, and protocols, she finds none, or if gaps abound, then a long-term goal might be to develop guidelines regarding use of college social media accounts. To ensure that all SGA members understand their responsibilities, Chandra might want to include social media as part of SGA training. Because social media have the power to reach countless constituents, Chandra might consider developing educational programs so that all

St. Andrews students, not just Jake and other SGA members, learn about responsible use of social media.

What impact will these outcomes have on the campus community? Through educational interventions, we hope that Jake, SGA members, and the general student body will be encouraged to self-monitor their (and their peers') social media behavior. Ideally, issues of responsibility, reputation, and community laced throughout the social media educational campaign would be transferrable to other campus issues and problems (e.g., underage drinking, civility).

Phase 2: Comprehensive Scan of Options

*Task: Evaluate preexisting/historical
solutions or design new solutions*

How has this type of problem been handled in the past at this institution or at another institution where you have worked? As Chandra collected information in Phase 1, she looked for policies, protocols, and precedent. In that process, she may have come across written documentation (or word of mouth) about how similar situations were handled at St. Andrews in the past. However, because the president only recently started following students on Twitter, the circumstances of this case are likely to be different than those in past situations. Other forms of damaging or inappropriate communications could have certainly occurred in cyberspace or other venues. Learning how St. Andrews dealt with critical student comments via the newspaper, posters, or other modes of communication might be useful.

Considering how similar problems have been handled at another institution might also be helpful. Other schools may have more experience responding to student use of social media, but Chandra should be careful about trying to adopt a plan that is not a good match for a religiously affiliated college; for instance, the treatment of similar situations at a large public institution with explicit social media policies might be quite different than how it could be successfully managed at St. Andrews. Campus context matters.

What protocols/guidelines/resources are available to handle this type of situation? As we evaluated options for Chandra, we agreed that a thorough review of campus protocols, policies, and precedent was warranted. One of the first things Chandra might want to look for is a campus protocol for responding to communications that could potentially damage the college's reputation. Does St. Andrews have one? Is it up to date? Does it cover communications by all constituents, including students? Similarly, she may want to review any protocols from the information technology office regarding use of college social media accounts.

Another place to look for guidelines or resources could be the student code of conduct. Does it include policies related to civil communications on campus? Is Jake's behavior a violation of campus policy or just poor judgment? Even if his behavior does not violate collegewide standards of student conduct, it might be a breach of SGA standards. Does the SGA have a handbook or constitution that explicates standards of behavior for student leaders? Do SGA materials offer guidelines for student use of SGA social media accounts? Any of these guidelines, policies, protocols, and resources may help Chandra as she considers her options.

What ideas are available from staff members, supervisors, or mentors about how to handle this situation? As is the case in most student affairs divisions, Chandra is probably surrounded by colleagues and senior staff who can provide guidance and support. Because Lynn is away and possibly not reachable, Chandra may receive no guidance from her direct supervisor. However, the dean of students will likely have suggestions for handling the situation. He might suggest options Chandra did not consider or offer valuable political insight. The dean also likely knows the president much better than Chandra does and might have ideas about what responses will be acceptable and unacceptable to Fr. Champlin.

In addition to senior staff, Chandra might have trusted colleagues or mentors who can offer insight into this situation. For instance, she might have a colleague who is an expert on Twitter. Or one of her colleagues might have a great relationship with Jake and have insight into how best to approach him.

What specific options are (or are not) available to you at this point? Once all the possible options are reviewed, Chandra must choose one. Ignoring the president's request is not an option—Chandra must handle the situation. If a specific protocol can be applied, she should follow it. Unless he is unreachable, meeting with Jake is also an option. She may not want, or have the authority, to take direct action (i.e., remove the offensive tweets or shut down the SGA Twitter account). After talking with the dean of students and IT personnel, Chandra will have a better sense of the technological options.

Task: Determine which options best match the desired outcomes

For each option, what barriers might prevent you from moving toward the desired outcomes? One option is to have an educational conversation with Jake. But Chandra might not be able to find Jake, or he might refuse to meet with her. If she does meet with him, she might not be able to get him to understand that his behavior was inappropriate. Hence, she may encounter a barrier in getting Jake to stop his profane and critical tweets.

If Chandra opts for an educational conversation with Jake rather than deleting offensive tweets or shutting down the account, she runs the risk of further angering the president. Since one of the decision-making goals (DMF, Phase 1) was to appease the president, the decision to be educational versus punitive might become a barrier to success. On the other hand, if Chandra decides that deleting tweets or temporarily turning off the SGA Twitter account was a reasonable course of action, she might not have the authority or access to do so.

Are there any constituents (student groups, parents, alumni, departments, staff, community members) who might be negatively affected by the choice of a particular option, thus impeding the desired outcome? How will you justify your choice to these constituents? Not removing offensive tweets or shutting down the Twitter account immediately might negatively affect admissions, especially if the incident occurs during the critical spring yield period. Similarly, the alumni office might be affected, especially if ensuing press discourages potential donors during a giving campaign. Finally, not taking direct action with the SGA Twitter account might anger the president, who suggested that Chandra do so. Justification to the president and these offices will likely involve a discussion about the importance of educational interventions with students and the hidden dangers of trying to stifle student use of social media. Ideally, the dean of students (whose support Chandra should gain *before* moving forward) will help convey these messages to stakeholders.

If Chandra chooses to and has the ability to delete tweets or turn off the Twitter account, the IT staff may be affected. They may have policies (or strong feelings) about who can intervene on university accounts and when it is appropriate to do so. If the president is adamant about having the account shut off, his office might contact the IT staff directly. Should Chandra decide that she does not want to turn off the account, but the president requests that IT do so, the IT staff will feel obligated to follow his directive.

Regardless of what Chandra decides, intradepartment dynamics could be affected. First, she has to make decisions in the absence of her supervisor. If Lynn disagrees with Chandra's tactics, the supervisor-supervisee relationship could be affected. Also, as Lynn is the co-advisor to the SGA, she might have strong feelings about Chandra making advising-related decisions in her absence. Chandra will need to be prepared to justify all her decisions upon her supervisor's return.

The student constituency, including the SGA, will likely be affected by Chandra's decision of whether or not to delete tweets or shut off the Twitter account. Such direct action on the account might temporarily stop the tweets, but it could anger the SGA and any other students who believe that their voices were stifled. Chandra's justification to these constituents should consider the developmental levels of the SGA members and the preexisting levels of trust in her relationship with that group.

If Chandra decides that education and policy change are essential, she may need to convince the students of the importance of such measures. While this incident needs a short-term solution, the long-term options should include education about the use of college social media accounts and the potential ramifications of leaving a less than positive digital footprint. It is hoped that such education will have a positive effect on Jake, the SGA, and the larger campus community.

Another goal for Chandra might be to create (or revise) policies regarding appropriate use of social media by students and student leaders. However, Jake, the SGA members, and other students might view education and policy changes as an infringement of their free speech and resist them. Chandra will have to be prepared to justify the importance of policy changes and educational initiatives to students.

What resources (e.g., financial, personnel) will you need to implement each option? If Chandra decides that educational programming for the entire student body is necessary, she will probably need some funding for publicity and implementation. She will also need personnel to assist with implementation. Experts on the power of social media (e.g., faculty members or staff in career services, technology, or public relations) might be helpful resources as she moves forward with an educational campaign. If she temporarily shuts off the SGA Twitter account, she will need the assistance of information technology personnel. As with most incidents, Chandra will need to draw on her own time, competencies, patience, and perseverance.

After weighing the pros and cons of each option, which one is most likely to move you toward your desired outcomes? The four authors decided that unless she was forced to do so by the president or the dean of students, we would not have Chandra delete tweets or suspend the SGA Twitter account. We preferred that she take the educational route rather than the punitive one. This would include an immediate educational conversation with Jake. The second aspect of the educational plan would be for Chandra to talk with the entire SGA about appropriate use of college social media accounts. As part of those discussions, Chandra would remind students about any existing SGA policies/ constitutional guidelines concerning responsible social media use or encourage the group to create new policies. Finally, we decided that Chandra's plan should include an educational campaign geared toward the entire student body about civility in online communications and the long-term consequences of inappropriate or unprofessional social media messages.

Phase 3: Implementation

Task: Move forward with your solution

What is your specific plan of action? The four authors decided that Chandra's specific plan of action would not include deleting tweets or suspending the SGA Twitter account. Instead, she would focus on educational interventions. Her first priority would be to meet with the dean of students to discuss the situation and her ideas. Once she has his support, she would have an educational conversation with Jake in hopes that the tweets would either cease or become more appropriate. Ideally, he would remove the offensive tweets. We would also like to see Chandra plan a series of educational programs for the SGA and the larger campus community about the potential implications on one's reputation and career of using social media. These educational events would include a variety of programs such as a presentation by career services about professional reputation; a dialogue with Fr. Champlin about religious perspectives on moral responsibility and reputation in a digital age; and a faculty-led program focused on civility, communication, and social responsibility. Chandra's plan would also include follow-up with the president.

What tasks must be accomplished to move forward with your plan? We recommend that Chandra engage in the following tasks as she moves forward with the plan:

- Contact her supervisor.
- Meet with the dean of students and garner support for the educational plan.

- Contact Jake to schedule a meeting.
- Contact information technology staff to ensure that they are aware of the plan of action.
- Schedule a meeting with the SGA.
- Follow up with the president.
- Connect with community partners who might be affected by this event (e.g., residence life, public safety, alumni relations, admissions, public relations).
- Plan educational events/speakers.

Who will perform the necessary tasks? Chandra herself will take on many of the tasks, including conversations with Jake, dialogues with the SGA, and outreach to program partners and affected constituents. Of course, during her conversation with the dean of students (and with Lynn, if she is reachable), the various tasks could be assigned differently. For instance, Lynn, who is the co-advisor of the SGA, might want Chandra to have an immediate conversation with Jake but wait to address the SGA until she returns. Lynn or the dean of students might also prefer that the outreach to other departments and faculty be done by someone in a more senior leadership position. For instance, the dean of students might prefer to connect with the leaders in admissions, alumni relations, and public relations. He and Lynn might also want to be the conduit for future communication with the president.

What is your prioritized time frame for each of these tasks? The time frame for each of Chandra's tasks is as follows:

- Immediately
  - ◊ Contact her supervisor.
  - ◊ Meet with the dean of students and garner support for the educational plan.

- ◊   After meeting with the dean of students, contact Jake to schedule a meeting.
- When appropriate
  - ◊   Contact information technology staff to ensure that they are aware of the plan of action.
- At the earliest opportunity
  - ◊   Schedule a meeting with the SGA.
- After discussions with the dean of students and Jake
  - ◊   Follow up with the president.
- Ongoing throughout the year
  - ◊   Connect with community partners who might be affected by this event (e.g., residence life, public safety, alumni relations, admissions, public relations).
  - ◊   Plan educational events/speakers.

Task: Possible reappraisal of your plan of action

What is your strategy for dealing with unforeseen issues, unintended consequences, or problems related to the implementation of your plan? As with any situation, there is always the possibility of unforeseen aspects of the problem or unintended consequences emerging. For instance, Chandra chooses not to delete critical tweets or suspend the Twitter account. Imagine that, before she can talk to Jake, he and other SGA members unleash a new barrage of foul-mouthed criticisms of the college. These tweets are re-tweeted and inspire other St. Andrews students to convey their dissatisfaction via personal social media accounts. The president is now even angrier. He calls the dean of students to ask why Chandra blatantly ignored his request.

Another unforeseen issue could be that the information technology staff shut off the Twitter account as directed by the president. Now Jake and the entire SGA are angry that freedom of speech has been stifled. Student leaders open an alternative SGA Twitter account and use personal accounts to spread the word about how St. Andrews is silencing students.

One strategy for dealing with these unforeseen issues and unintended consequences is for Chandra to revisit the DMF regularly. In chapter 2, we explained that the DMF is not perfectly linear; rather, it is iterative. Chandra may need to revisit different phases as she works through complex situations like this one. For instance, if the SGA account is suspended by IT services, she will still have to continue her educational efforts. If the evolving problem includes a student protest, her options will have to include managing the anger of SGA members and other students who feel silenced by college actions.

Is your initial appraisal of the problem on target, or does the problem need to be reappraised? In a case study simulation, this question is somewhat difficult to answer. Given the answers to the previous questions, the initial appraisal might be on track. If any of the answers were different, it might need to be revisited. For instance, when she was gathering information, Chandra might have found that Jake did not post the tweets. Did someone without proper access post those tweets? If so, St. Andrews might have an information technology security issue on its hands. If the tweets were a joke by a fellow SGA member, the solutions might need to include a clarification of SGA roles and trust building among student leaders. Or Chandra might reappraise the problem if she found that the tweets were relatively benign. In that case, her understanding of the potential public relations problem might be altered.

Are there any changes in your plan or strategy at this point? It is impossible to accurately assess unintended consequences or unforeseen circumstances in a simulated case study. In this sample case, we would not suggest that Chandra alter her initial strategy. In real life, however, decision makers may indeed need to change strategy to deal with unintended consequences, unforeseen circumstances, or new information.

Phase 4: Assessment

Phase 4 of the DMF is a final assessment of the decision-making process and the outcomes, in which decision makers reflect on the success or failure of their actions. Specifically, decision makers need to consider whether the outcomes determined in Phase 1 were achieved. And beyond outcomes, decision makers need to assess and learn from their process. A candid assessment of skills and shortcomings can help novice and seasoned decision makers more effectively manage future problems and crises.

Because Phase 4 is integral to the DMF, we decided that it was imperative to include assessment in our sample case study. Therefore, we intentionally selected the "To Tweet or Not to Tweet" case because it is based on a real-life situation. In the interest of confidentiality, the institution, names, and a few facts were changed. In this section, we summarize Chandra's actual response to the case and her real-life assessment situation. By selecting an incident that actually occurred on a college campus, we are able to summarize how Phase 4 can be applied to decision-making outcomes and processes.

Task: Reflect on the impact and success of your solutions

Were the desired outcomes achieved? In the actual incident, some of the outcomes were fully achieved, while others were only partially accomplished. At St. Andrews College, the real Chandra decided on three desired outcomes. The first was to persuade the president not to shut down the SGA social media accounts, which he threatened to do. The second was to convince the president that taking an educational approach with Jake and the SGA was the best way to resolve the matter. The president agreed to both requests, but he was emphatic that the negative comments and inappropriate language on all college-related social media, including Twitter, must stop immediately.

Chandra's third desired outcome was that the foul-mouthed tweets would stop and Jake would understand that his actions had consequences. The meeting with Jake did not go as well as she hoped. Jake adamantly argued that he had the right to say what he wanted on Twitter. Despite a lengthy discussion, he did not seem to understand why his actions were inappropriate. Jake continued to use foul-mouthed criticisms on his personal Twitter account, but he did comply with the request to stop using profanity on the SGA Twitter account. At first, Chandra thought she had achieved only a partial victory, as Jake's sense of responsibility as a student leader and his personal social media behavior did not immediately change. However, when Jake began his job search the following semester, he deleted many of his inappropriate tweets. It seemed that he had learned a lesson after all.

Chandra did not initially set as a desired long-term outcome students gaining an understanding of the potential impact of social media on their careers and reputations. Instead, her focus was on education for Jake and other SGA members. However, her perspective changed as she navigated the unanticipated outcomes.

Do any unanticipated outcomes need to be addressed? Jake's initial reaction was unanticipated—Chandra was disappointed that he continued the negative tweets on his personal account. Another unanticipated outcome was the mixed response from members of the SGA—the group was split on whether Jake's behavior was appropriate.

As a result of these outcomes, Chandra decided that comprehensive education for both student leaders and students in general about the appropriate use of social media was imperative.

Two other issues emerged as the situation evolved. One was a concern about drinking on campus. Initially, Chandra did not consider Jake's behavior as a reinforcement of an unhealthy drinking culture. The second unforeseen issue had to do with student perceptions that public safety and residence life were being aggressive in their interactions with students, especially when alcohol was involved. At her meeting with the SGA, student leaders cited a number of incidents in which public safety and residence life staff reacted overzealously and were sometimes exceedingly harsh with students. These issues were brought to the attention of the dean of students.

In the case study and in real life, Chandra wondered about the potential of Jake's tweets to cause a social media rant by students. A negative Twitter campaign by students could have affected alumni, prospective students, and parents. Luckily, this did not happen in real life.

In her search for protocols, guidelines, and precedents, Chandra found that St. Andrews had none. Thus, an emergent desired outcome was to work with campus constituents to develop policies and guidelines regarding expectations for appropriate use of college social media accounts.

With whom did you consult to determine the impact of your plan/ solution? Chandra discussed her desired outcomes and plans for implementation with Lynn, the director of student activities, upon her return; with the dean of students; and with other directors in the student affairs division. She also communicated with colleagues in admissions, information technology, and college advancement. (In real life, the conversations with other directors were led by the dean of students, not by Chandra.) Although the campus context of St. Andrews was one in which the chain of command was regularly ignored, the dean of students decided that it should be more closely followed in situations that involved the president. The dean accompanied Chandra to the follow-up meeting with the president.

Overwhelmingly, the parties involved agreed that the effect of Chandra's decision making was mostly positive. All constituents were pleased that the profanity-laden tweets ceased on the college account. They were also happy that some educational conversations about responsible use of social media had begun with Jake and the SGA. Everyone, including the president, agreed on the need to formalize guidelines for the use of college social media accounts.

Task: Reflect on your implementation process and new learning

What can you learn from your mistakes and successes? While decision makers can learn from both successes and mistakes, the latter are typically more memorable. Chandra learned the importance of understanding campus politics. As a new professional, she assumed that most St. Andrews employees, including the president, were as familiar with Twitter as she was. She understood the frequency with which students made inappropriate comments on Twitter and was caught off guard by Fr. Champlin's surprise at Jake's behavior. She learned not to make assumptions about the technological savvy of colleagues. This was not a mistake as much as it was an oversight; however, in decision making, oversights can hinder success.

Chandra also learned that information gathering can uncover a multitude of related problems. By employing effective listening skills as she gathered information, Chandra learned about animosity and lack of trust between students and two key departments: residence life and public safety. Had she not been thoughtful in her communication with students, this information might not have come to light. When she passed it along to the dean of students, he was very concerned. He saw animosity between students and staff as antithetical to a healthy and educational climate at St. Andrews, and took action to address this unanticipated but important issue.

Chandra's conversations with SGA members also brought out the need for campuswide education on the use of social media. During Phase 3, she realized that her initial strategy to educate only Jake and the SGA was shortsighted. The SGA members' lack of understanding about the ramifications of inappropriate use of social media reflected a problem in the student body as a whole and called for additional strategies. Chandra successfully used the DMF as an iterative process and decided that campuswide education about social media use was warranted. She and her colleagues planned a number of events to meet this need, and the dean of students worked with faculty to introduce the topic of responsible social media use into the curriculum.

As she reflected on her process, Chandra considered the success of her educational conversation with Jake. While he agreed to stop the negative tweets on the SGA account, he continued to post profanity-laden tweets on his personal account. Chandra wondered if her educational tactics were effective. Would Jake have learned more if she had taken a different approach? As the year progressed, Chandra was reminded that education and growth take time, and that she may have planted a seed that eventually changed the way Jake thought about his freedom to tweet. While Chandra will never know the true extent of his learning, Jake did alter his behavior later to avoid damaging his reputation during the job search process.

What might you do differently next time? In real life, Chandra was well aware of many instances of inappropriate Twitter use by students, so she did not initially understand why the president was so upset. In fact, at first she took the president's request somewhat lightly and did not plan to deal with the issue immediately. However, her discussion with the dean of students made Chandra understand that the situation was politically urgent; therefore, she followed the dean's advice to resolve the matter at once. Next time, Chandra will know that it is important to deal with a presidential request immediately.

In the real-life situation, Chandra did not consider how social media were connected to the overall level of student civility or the possible perpetuation of a party culture at St. Andrews. Nor did she initially plan educational interventions for the larger campus community. The next time Chandra determines that student leaders are in need of education about a topic, she may also think about how the general student body could also benefit from such initiatives.

What did you learn about your own decision-making style? How might this new knowledge help you in the future? Learning to read the urgency in others was a major discovery for Chandra. Even though the situation did not seem urgent to her, it was extremely urgent to the president. Chandra learned that she needs to consider others' perspectives on significance and urgency in decision making. The initial interaction with Fr. Champlin also taught Chandra that professionals take different approaches to the same situation. His suggestion of shutting off the Twitter account was in stark contrast to her ideas about educating Jake and other SGA leaders. This situation also taught her that some professionals may not see the benefits of selecting educational versus punitive responses. In future situations, Chandra will be more prepared to convey her educational approach and rationalize her decisions to those with less developmental perspectives.

Finally, Chandra learned how to effectively communicate her ideas and implement a decision that was very different than the punitive approach the president wanted to take. While the outcome was successful in this case, Chandra reflected on how adopting a strategy that does not align with the approach of senior officials might not always be the wise choice.

What policies, programs, or protocols need to be reviewed or put into place to prevent similar situations from occurring in the future? Chandra determined that St. Andrews did not have any policies or guidelines for social media use. As the situation evolved, she began to see a need for social media guidelines and policies not only for students but for all parties at the college. In conversations with the dean of students, the director of student activities, and the president, it became apparent that these new policies should include an emphasis on civility and mutual respect toward others as well as a certain level of deference to the college. St. Andrews strives to foster a spirit of community, loyalty, and pride. Chandra learned that any new policies and guidelines had to align with this campus context.

In the real-life situation, the St. Andrews student code of conduct and the *Employee and Faculty Handbook* were amended with statements regarding appropriate use of social media. Both documents now describe specific consequences for violation of the social media policies. The moral clause in the student government constitution was also revised to include expectations about responsible use of social media.

Competencies Matter

In the introduction, we stated our belief that all 10 of the professional competency areas (ACPA & NASPA, 2010) connect to the daily work of student affairs professionals. As practitioners such as Chandra encounter situations like "To Tweet or Not to Tweet," they may find that certain competency areas are exceedingly relevant while other areas are less so. In the following pages, we explain how all 10 of the competency areas might relate to this case study. While we cannot provide an exhaustive discussion of the competencies, the following paragraphs are intended to explicate how professionals like Chandra can reflect on and hone their professional competencies as they make decisions about contemporary student affairs problems.

Advising and Helping

A variety of basic and intermediate competencies could be relevant to this case. First, as Chandra engaged in conversations with Jake about his behavior, she may have used many of the 13 basic advising and helping competencies, such as effective listening skills and nonverbal communication, establishing rapport, and facilitating Jake's reflection by using appropriate challenge and support. Chandra may also have found some of the intermediate-level competencies useful when she met with the SGA to discuss, develop, and implement revisions to the student government constitution. During conversations with Jake and the SGA, Chandra might have had to "perceive and analyze unspoken dynamics in a group setting" and "facilitate or coach group decision-making, goal-setting, and process" (ACPA & NASPA, 2010, p. 6).

Assessment, Evaluation, and Research

Two basic assessment, evaluation, and research competencies could be relevant to this case study. First, professionals are expected to "effectively articulate, interpret, and use results of assessment, evaluation, and research reports and studies, including professional literature" (ACPA & NASPA, 2010, p. 8). Was Chandra familiar with the research on social media use in higher education? Literature on the legal and ethical issues related to social media use might prove exceptionally helpful in the future as Chandra navigates similar situations. At the intermediate level, Chandra's long-range educational plans might have included assessment. To plan effective educational programs for students, Chandra might assess their current levels of knowledge regarding the dangers and benefits of expressing themselves and posting personal information on the Internet. She might also propose an assessment of the campus drinking culture. If her supervisor and the dean of students are interested in such an assessment, Chandra might "construct basic surveys and other instruments with consultation" (ACPA & NASPA, 2010, p. 8).

Equity, Diversity, and Inclusion

In this case, issues of racial, gender, sexual, class, or other forms of discrimination were not readily apparent. But they certainly could have been uncovered as Chandra read the tweets and talked with key stakeholders. One of the foundations of an equitable environment is that diverse views and backgrounds are validated and, in turn, enrich the learning environment. Although it is a Catholic institution, St. Andrews enrolls students from a host of religious and spiritual backgrounds, and even among Catholic students, religious diversity likely exists. A basic skill in the equity, diversity, and inclusion competency area that applies to this scenario is the need to "identify the contributions of similar and diverse peoples within and to the institutional environment" (ACPA & NASPA, 2010, p. 10). In the case, Fr. Champlin saw Jake's tweets as an affront to Catholic values. To make effective decisions in a case like this, Chandra may need to assess how other stakeholders (e.g., current students, alumni, donors, prospective students, and parents) view the tweets.

Ethical Professional Practice

Ethical issues were not at the forefront of Chandra's mind in this situation. However, as she used Phase 4 to reflect on her outcomes and process, she pondered why ethical issues did *not* occur to her. In doing so, she was tapping into a basic-level skill to "identify ethical issues in the course of one's job" (ACPA & NASPA, 2010, p. 12). If Chandra had determined that the situation was an ethical one, she might have had to "explain how one's behavior embodies the ethical statements of the profession, particularly in relationships with students and colleagues, in the use of technology" (ACPA & NASPA, 2010, p. 12).

History, Philosophy, and Values

The president suggested that Chandra shut down the Twitter account, but she believed that suspending the account was not the most developmental approach to the situation. While Fr. Champlin was thinking about the reputation of the school, Chandra's educational response was rooted in the history, philosophy, and values of the student affairs profession, including the basic competency to "demonstrate empathy and compassion for student needs" (ACPA & NASPA, 2010, p. 14). That is not to say that Chandra did not consider the school's reputation, but that consideration did not subsume her developmental focus.

In her conversations with students, Chandra found that Jake and his peers needed developmental interventions. As she progressed through her decision-making process, Chandra had the opportunity to "model the principles of the profession and communicate the expectation of the same from colleagues and supervisees" (ACPA & NASPA, 2010, p. 14), which is another basic competency in this area.

Human and Organizational Resources

The human and organizational resources competency area encapsulates a variety of skills, including supervision, conflict management, and political navigation. In this case, Chandra was dealing with conflicting views and was enmeshed in campus politics. As part of her decision-making process, she searched for relevant protocols, guidelines, and precedent. This portion of the DMF aligns with the basic human and organizational resources competency to "describe campus protocols for responding to significant incidents and campus crises" (ACPA & NASPA, 2010, p. 16). An equally relevant competency in this case is to "maintain a level of technical knowledge that allows one to effectively use existing technologies as well as to incorporate new emerging technologies as they may benefit one's work" (ACPA & NASPA, 2010, p. 17). If Chandra had no idea what Twitter was or how it worked, she would need some professional development in this competency area.

Law, Policy, and Governance

As she responded to the incident, Chandra may have asked, "Can Jake legally do that?" If she did, she may have been tapping into basic competencies in the law, policy, and governance area. For instance, professionals should be able to "explain the differences between public and private higher education with respect to the legal system and what they may mean for students, faculty, and staff at both types of institutions" (ACPA & NASPA, 2010, p. 20). Because St. Andrews is a private, religiously affiliated college, Chandra's response to questions of legality would need to be informed by this contextual reality.

Leadership

The "To Tweet or Not to Tweet" situation afforded Chandra the opportunity to consider a variety of basic leadership competencies. First, good leaders can "identify institutional traditions, mores, and organizational structures (e.g., hierarchy, networks, governing groups, nature of power, policies, goals, agendas and resource allocation processes) and how they influence others to act in the organization" (ACPA & NASPA, 2010, p. 22). This situation was laden with politics, hierarchy, and power, and Chandra effectively identified some, but not all, of these leadership issues.

A related competency in the leadership area suggests that professionals "identify and then effectively consult with key stakeholders and those with diverse perspectives to make informed decisions" (ACPA & NASPA, 2010, p. 22). The key stakeholders in this case included the president, the dean of students, the director of student activities, and other campus officials who may have been affected by the tweets (e.g., residence life, admissions, alumni affairs). Chandra identified many of these constituents and worked with the dean of students to effectively consult with them.

Effective decision makers can "articulate the logic used in making decisions to all interested parties" (ACPA & NASPA, 2010, p. 22). Indeed, one of the DMF questions in Phase 2 asks decision makers to consider how to justify their choices to various constituents. While the ability to articulate logic is always important, it is imperative in cases such as this one, where the plan of action (i.e., not to shut off the Twitter account) runs counter to the suggestion of the president. Chandra had to effectively communicate her plan with both the dean of students and the president, and explain why her plan should be implemented. However, as an entry-level professional, she also needed to understand that if her desired course of action was not supported by her superiors, she would have had little choice but to implement the wishes of the president. One aspect of good leadership is knowing when to follow.

Personal Foundations

A situation like the one in "To Tweet or Not to Tweet" can elicit a variety of emotions. Because Chandra disagreed with the president's suggestion to shut down the Twitter account, her personal foundations may have been shaken. One of the basic competencies in this area is to "identify key elements of one's set of personal beliefs and commitments (e.g., values, morals, goals, desires, self-definitions), as well as the source of each (e.g., self, peers, family, or one or more larger communities)" (ACPA & NASPA, 2010, p. 24). In a situation like this, Chandra might need to identify the elements of her personal values, morals, desires, and self-definitions. How did she feel about social media, student development, and disagreeing with a senior leader? This competency area suggests that practitioners "recognize the importance of reflection in personal and professional development" (ACPA & NASPA, 2010, p. 24). Reflection is built into all the DMF key questions and considerations, and is the bedrock of Phase 4. People who engage in regular and candid self-reflection may also be able to "explain the process for executing responsibilities dutifully and thoughtfully" (ACPA & NASPA, 2010, p. 25), which is one of the intermediate competencies in this area. In this case, Chandra may have had to explain how she executed her responsibilities as the assistant director of student activities in a dutiful and thoughtful manner.

Student Learning and Development

At the heart of student affairs work is a focus on student learning and development. It is imperative that professionals master the basic-level competency to "articulate theories and models that describe the development of college students and the conditions and practices that facilitate holistic development" (ACPA & NASPA, 2010, p. 26). A number of developmental theories (e.g., moral, psychosocial, cognitive, typological) could have been useful as Chandra worked with Jake and other SGA members. In the case study, her long-term plans included promoting responsible use of social media through an educational campaign. As she planned these initiatives, she was "design[ing] programs and services to promote student learning and development," which is an intermediate-level competency (ACPA & NASPA, 2010, p. 26).

Summary

In this chapter, the four authors applied the DMF to a sample case to illustrate the decision-making process. The conversation was rich with discussion and debate, and gave us the opportunity to move step by step through the DMF as our readers would ultimately do. Using the DMF, we identified the problem, scanned options, and anticipated the possibility of implementing plans for a resolution of the problem. Because the case was based on a real event, we were also able to provide insight into Chandra's assessment of her process and outcomes. Finally, we related the case to each of the 10 competency areas to emphasize the connection between decision making and competency development. We hope this chapter will serve as a helpful example as you apply the DMF to the cases in chapter 4 and to real-life situations.

REFERENCES

American College Personnel Association (ACPA) and National Association of Student Personnel Administrators (NASPA). (2010). *Professional competency areas for student affairs practitioners.* Retrieved from http://www.naspa.org/programs/prodev/Professional_Competencies.pdf

Hutchens, N. (2012). You can't post that . . . or can you? Legal issues related to college and university students' online free speech. *Journal of Student Affairs Research and Practice, 49*(1), 1–15.

CHAPTER 4

Case Studies

IN THE PREVIOUS chapters, we summarized the literature on decision making, introduced you to the decision-making framework (DMF), and applied the framework to a sample case study. Now, it is your turn to apply the DMF to contemporary student affairs problems. In this chapter, we offer 30 case study situations. For reasons of confidentiality, the identities of individuals and institutions in the cases have been changed. The case studies in this chapter are organized in alphabetical order. If you are interested in a case study that highlights particular competency areas, institution types, functional areas, or subjects, the cases are grouped accordingly in the list of cases at the end of the book. Once you have chosen your case, we encourage you to use the DMF insert as a guide as you determine the nature of a problem, scan for possible solutions, enact methods of implementation, and assess the effectiveness of your decision-making process.

Although the cases in this chapter can be analyzed independently, we suggest that small groups of practitioners collaboratively work through each scenario. Administrative working groups might convene to discuss the scenarios for training purposes, or faculty might use them to facilitate discussion in the classroom. Each person brings a unique set of perspectives, experiences, and paradigms to the decision-making process. When multiple people analyze a single case study, learning from each other's perspectives becomes part of the educational process. As the four authors applied the DMF to the sample case in chapter 3, we learned from our differences. We hope that you, too, will learn from classmates and colleagues as you use the DMF to grapple with the contemporary case studies in this chapter.

Your experience, perspective, and institutional context will shape the way you respond to the DMF questions. At different moments in our careers, we are a unique mix of developmental levels (e.g., cognitive, psychosocial, moral). While student affairs professionals are taught to acknowledge the varying developmental needs of students, we sometimes forget that lifespan developmental theories apply to all of us—as we grow and develop, our perspective changes. As you progress along your developmental trajectory, gain professional experience, and explore various theoretical paradigms, you will likely find yourself answering the DMF questions differently. Should you revisit these case studies in the future, your responses might be quite different than they are today.

As you read through the cases, pay attention to context. Most cases are situated in a particular institutional and community context, and those contexts should inform how you proceed with your analysis. It is easy to slip into responding to the DMF questions in a way that aligns with the campus and community contexts of your current assistantship, internship, or professional position. For example, if you work at a large, public institution where there is a lack of protocols, much political strife, and an expectation that entry-level staff include supervisors in all decisions, your responses to the DMF questions are likely to be shaped by those realities. Try to remember that the environmental contexts of the case studies (and of real-world situations) are bound by location and time. To be most effective in decision making, you must be able to recognize and analyze the most appropriate contexts for the situation at hand.

Another caveat is that for any complex problem, there may be a number of good solutions. Case studies allow you to learn about, practice, and reflect on your decision-making process (and potential outcomes) in collaboration with peers and colleagues. The case studies are not tests to determine whether you made the "right" decision. Rarely is there only one correct way to solve a problem. Instead, the cases are a training ground for you to learn and practice reflective decision making.

As we noted earlier, it is difficult to complete a thorough assessment (Phase 4) with case simulations. Despite the centrality of Phase 4 to the DMF, it is impossible to conduct an accurate assessment of outcomes when you are working with a case study. Therefore, as you use the DMF to work through the following cases, you might not be able to accomplish the first task in Phase 4, which is to "reflect on the impact and success of your solutions." Outcomes cannot be assessed in a fictitious case because they did not happen. But we strongly encourage you to engage in such reflection as you encounter real-world problems. The second task in Phase 4—"reflect on your implementation process and new learning"—can be completed in both real-life and case study scenarios. As you work through the cases with peers and colleagues, be sure to think about what you learned from the collaborative decision-making process.

Each case study includes two sections: Context Matters and Competencies Matter. In the Context Matters section, we pose questions that could change the context of the case study scenario, then ask you to consider whether and how your decision making might be altered to adapt to the different context. In the Competencies Matter section, we list a few competency areas that relate to the case and describe how a professional in a similar situation could draw on selected basic and intermediate professional competencies (ACPA & NASPA, 2010). After our discussion, we invite you to imagine how other competencies might also apply to the case. Decisions matter, but context and competencies matter too.

Both/And

You work in the Transfer Services Department at a midsize community college in the Northwest. In addition to your paid position, you volunteer as the staff advisor to a student group on campus called Both/And. The group has approximately 10 members who attend meetings regularly. Recently, the group has been discussing some racial incidents on campus. Group members are dismayed by racist graffiti and concerned about the invisibility of biracial and multiracial people at the community college.

In response to a recent bias incident on campus, Dr. Smith, president of the college, says she will dedicate a portion of a $250,000 donation to address climate issues on campus. She plans to systematically assess the issues and appropriate resources where they will have the biggest impact. Dr. Smith directs the assessment office to conduct a campus climate survey. The questionnaire asks about a variety of issues related to race, ability, gender, and social class. The demographic section of the questionnaire asks respondents to select their race, but it does not offer a category for biracial or multiracial people, nor are respondents able to select more than one box to indicate their race.

Members of Both/And are outraged that the questionnaire does not acknowledge the existence of biracial and multiracial students, especially because they know that resources will be tied to questionnaire findings. Both/And had high hopes that some of the funding would be used to expand the multicultural center services and programs to be more inclusive of biracial and multiracial students. Without asking biracial and multiracial students about their experiences, it will be impossible for the university to know what kinds of services and programs they need.

You receive a call from John, the vice president of the Both/And group, who tells you that the group is planning to stage a protest in the president's office the next day. You are on the phone with John when your supervisor, Kate, enters your office. Kate is concerned that you are spending office time on Both/And business. You tell her that this is a unique situation and fill her in on group concerns and protest plans. Kate suggests that you have gotten yourself into a tough situation. She reminds you that you are a college employee and you should not act in a manner that suggests that you are in disagreement with the president's actions. When you mention that you, too, are concerned about the lack of inclusion of biracial and multiracial demographics on the survey, Kate remarks that you might be overreacting because the topic is "too personal" because of your own racial background. She says that she was concerned because sexual orientation was not included in the climate survey; however, she believes it is not her role—or yours—to allow personal perspectives to influence behavior at work.

Using Phases 1–3 of the DMF, how would you respond? First consider the case as written, and then revisit your decisions in light of the different contexts described below.

CONTEXT MATTERS (PROFESSIONAL/CAMPUS/COMMUNITY)

1. What if your campus had not had any recent racial incidents?
2. What if, on your annual performance evaluation, your supervisor rated you low on professionalism, commenting that you tended to get too personally involved in campus incidents?
3. What if this institution were a historically Black college or university (HBCU) or a Hispanic-serving institution (HSI)?

COMPETENCIES MATTER

The first competency area that could be related to this case is **assessment, evaluation, and research.** One of the intermediate competencies is to "use culturally relevant and culturally appropriate terminology and methods to conduct and report AER [assessment, evaluation, and research] findings" (ACPA & NASPA, 2010, p. 8). In this case, the assessment office did not use culturally inclusive methods. The inability of biracial and multiracial people to self-identify on the survey limits the usefulness of the data. In effect, the instrument provides no data to help professionals understand the unique needs of students who identify with more than one racial group. Because of the way the assessment instrument was constructed, their needs and experiences are invisible.

While you cannot turn back the hands of time and recreate the survey, what actions might you take to ensure that future assessments are more inclusive? Is there a way to augment the survey findings with data from biracial and multiracial people on campus? How might you use your **assessment, evaluation, and research** competencies to do so? For instance, you might "apply the concepts and procedures of qualitative research, evaluation, and assessment" (ACPA & NASPA, 2010, p. 9) to conduct focus groups with biracial and multiracial people on campus, or encourage the assessment office to do so. If it is not possible to conduct more campuswide assessment, how can you work within the scope of your role to ensure that the voices of biracial and multiracial students are included in departmental decision making? A helpful resource might be the *New Directions for Student Services* volume on biracial and multiracial students (Renn & Shang, 2008).

A related intermediate *equity, diversity, and inclusion* competency is to "identify systemic barriers to equality and inclusiveness, then advocate for and implement means of dismantling them" (ACPA & NASPA, 2010, p. 11). In this case, you may have determined that the assessment and the corresponding appropriation of funds are barriers to equality on campus. Phase 1 of the DMF invites you to consider your role and power in a situation. What do you think your role is in this case? How is your view of your role similar to or different from that of your supervisor? What are the implications of having differing perspectives?

In this scenario, you are likely considering the *personal foundations* intermediate skill to "recognize the effect between one's professional and personal lives, and develop plans to manage any related concerns" (ACPA & NASPA, 2010, p. 24). This case highlights some potential intersections between your personal and professional lives. Some higher education professionals believe that these intersections are important; many even argue that using our personal lives to inform our professional work is authentic and positive. Others—like your supervisor in this case—firmly believe that professional and personal lives should remain separate. How might you manage these intersections? What feels right for you? How does your decision to keep your personal and professional lives connected or separate fit with the culture of your office and institution? If there is incongruence, is it reconcilable? If not, what will you do? As you answer these questions, we hope that you return to the questions in Phase 1 of the DMF; for instance, "What do the parties involved see as the problem?" and "How are they handling their involvement in the problem?" As an entry-level employee, these questions should inform your decision-making process. The perspectives of those around you, including your supervisor, must inform your process.

What other competencies might be relevant to this scenerio and your decision-making process?

Brianna's Boyfriend

You are working at Ochre State College, a midsize institution of 5,000 students. Ochre's student body is very diverse, and the college offers many different support services. You are an academic advisor—you provide guidance to students on course selection.

Brianna Bellos is one of your advisees. She is a junior, very involved, and loves to talk about her boyfriend, Sean. In your first meeting with Brianna, she tells you that she and Sean have been together for 6 months and she thinks he is "the one." Sean attends a college in another state, but they maintain a long-distance relationship.

About halfway through the semester, Brianna arrives at your office completely distraught. On Facebook, she saw that Sean had been tagged in a photo kissing another girl. Brianna has tried to text him, but he is not responding. She cannot believe he has cheated on her and does not know what to do. She says she has not been eating or sleeping, has been missing classes and not completing her academic work, and feels that she cannot function until she learns the truth.

As she tells you more about her relationship with Sean, you learn that Brianna and Sean have never met in person. They became friends on Facebook and later started connecting via text messaging, FaceTime, and Twitter. She said they had hoped to meet soon, and she knew in her heart that he was the person for her. Now, she does not know what to do. She would travel to see him, but her parents refuse to give her the money, because they do not think it would be safe. "Besides," she says, "they do not think it is a real relationship." She plans to borrow a friend's car and drive out to see him. She wants to know if the college will give her a leave of absence so she can go.

Using Phases 1–3 of the DMF, how would you respond? First consider the case as written, and then revisit your decisions in light of the different contexts described below.

CONTEXT MATTERS (PROFESSIONAL/CAMPUS/COMMUNITY)

1. What if Sean contacts Orche's public safety office and informs them that Brianna is sending him text messages indicating that she is going to kill herself?
2. What if Brianna's mother attended your meeting and fully supports Brianna's request for a leave of absence so she can go see Sean?
3. What if you learn that Sean feels that he is being stalked by Brianna and has obtained a restraining order against her?

COMPETENCIES MATTER

In the context of using the Internet as an intermediary for dating, Brianna's behavior is not uncommon among the traditional-age college population. However, the possibility of her being exposed to a risky situation or being inappropriately engaged in online behaviors that may be emotionally risky makes an appraisal of the urgency or threat in this case a consideration in Phase 1 of the DMF. In fact, in one study, as many as 54% of late adolescents' online profiles included content that suggested risky behaviors related to sex or drug use (Pujazon-Zazik, Manasse, & Orrell-Valente, 2012). Additionally, because online daters often present themselves in more positive ways than their true identities would warrant (Ellison, Hancock, & Toma, 2012), it is reasonable to ask questions about Sean during Phase 1.

In this case, it would be imperative to be able to identify patterns of behavior that signal mental health concerns, a paramount skill in the *advising and helping* competency area (ACPA & NASPA, 2010). Stevens and Morris (2007) observed that lack of a romantic attachment may be a significant factor in the development of social and mental health problems. They also noted that dating anxiety may play a role in participation in online dating. In their study of online relationships, they found that 70% of online involvements resulted in face-to-face meetings. Undoubtedly, having a background in mental health issues would be an asset for you in your work; at the very least, some training in assessment of mental health concerns would provide you with a starting point in assessing the problem.

Lacking this foundation, you would need to know and use referral sources (e.g., other offices, outside agencies, and knowledge sources) and to seek expert assistance, which is another basic-level skill in the *advising and helping* competency area (ACPA & NASPA, 2010). These are major steps for you as you proceed through Phase 1 of the DMF from identifying the problem to determining desired outcomes. Do you have concerns about Brianna's capacity to determine the safety of this experience or her ability to handle the emotions associated with the rejection? Is the desired outcome in this case that she be protected from potential harm in going to meet Sean or that she develop a healthier approach to relationships? Is academic success your primary goal for Brianna?

As with other advising cases of this nature, your concern may also be about confidentiality, and you would need to rely on other competencies in *advising and helping*, such as to "maintain an appropriate degree of confidentiality that follows applicable legal and licensing requirements, facilitates the development of trusting relationships, and recognizes when confidentiality should be broken to protect the student or others" (ACPA & NASPA, 2010, p. 6). As you scan the options (DMF, Phase 2) and decide whether you should communicate with Brianna's parents about the possibility of her going to meet this young man, you may have to consider available protocols for handling this type of situation. The National Academic Advising Association (NACADA) recommends that "advisors respect student confidentiality rights regarding personal information. Advisors [should] practice with an understanding of the institution's interpretation of applicable laws, such as the Family Educational Rights and Privacy Act [FERPA]" (NACADA, 2012). Having knowledge of FERPA and applying it to your decision making in this case are important *law, policy, and governance* competencies (ACPA & NASPA, 2010). What other legal or policy issues might come into play in your decision?

What other competencies might be relevant to this scenerio and your decision-making process?

Bulking Up

You are the athletic academic advisor for a National Collegiate Athletic Association (NCAA) Division II football team at Agile University, a medium-sized private institution. The football team is the pride of this institution—it not only brings in significant revenues to the university but is also a source of substantial enrollments. The university is tuition-driven and has only a small endowment to offset operating costs; hence, there is a great deal of pressure to attract and retain students. Rising tuition costs have reduced the number of applicants each year, but surveys have shown that one of the main reasons students choose to attend the institution is because of the strong sense of spirit that pervades the campus, created by the excitement and the sense of school identity derived from sports, particularly football. Donors to the alumni fund frequently mention connections to sports programs as one incentive for their giving.

Your role as an athletic academic advisor is to provide academic coaching and support through weekly one-on-one meetings with football team members. There is one other athletic academic advisor for the football team. In your role, you also provide counseling for issues that might affect sports performance and monitor the academic progress of team members. You report to the athletic director of the university, whose department falls under the Division of Student Affairs. Although you are paid through the athletics department, you work closely with academic affairs to develop academic plans and monitor student progress. While some faculty members support athletes, others are less enamored with their "celebrity" and resist academic adaptations for them (e.g., schedules, assignment due dates, make-up work). You are often in the position of having to put a positive spin on athletics to gain the support of these less-than-enthusiastic professors.

In the middle of your (winning) football season, one of your players, a junior, has come to you with a complaint that he is not being given the opportunity to play because the starter who is ahead of him has been using steroids. The player tells you that he does not want to get the starting player in trouble, but it is not fair to have to sit on the bench because the other player is using steroids. He says, "I play clean; why should I suffer?" He implies that other players are doping as well. The specific player he is talking about is an advisee of the other athletic academic advisor.

Using Phases 1–3 of the DMF, how would you respond? First consider the case as written, and then revisit your decisions in light of the different contexts described below.

Context Matters (Professional/Campus/Community)

1. What if you are in this role at a nationally known NCAA Division I school?
2. What if, instead of steroid violations, the student athlete tells you that two of the star players are being given academic privileges and accommodations so they will not lose eligibility?

3. What if the student tells you that he has already reported this to the coach, and the coach has not done anything about it?

COMPETENCIES MATTER

The issues involved in this case require basic competencies in ***ethical professional practice***, particularly to "articulate one's personal code of ethics for student affairs practice, which reflects the ethical statements of professional student affairs associations and their foundational ethical principles" (ACPA & NASPA, 2010, p. 12). Intermediate competencies to "identify and seek to resolve areas of incongruence between personal, institutional, and professional ethical standards" are also essential for effective decision making in this situation (ACPA & NASPA, 2010, p. 12).

As you define the problem (DMF, Phase 1) in this case, you must first determine your role in the situation. As an academic advisor for athletes, you are challenged by potential ethical conflicts in both the academic and athletic arenas. You might have to address actions that are not consistent with ethical standards or regulations of your institution or with professional development organizations. The National Association of Academic Advisors for Athletics (N4A), for example, requires members to "ensure that the Athletic Advising Program is in compliance with academic requirements of the NCAA, NAIA [National Association of Intercollegiate Athletics], NJCAA [National Junior College Athletic Association] or any other associational governing body, as well as any conference standards or requirements of the particular institution" (N4A, 2012, p. 4). Also, the National Academic Advising Association (NACADA, 2012) suggests that advisors are responsible to their institutions and must uphold the specific policies, procedures, and values of their departments and institutions. In defining the problem (DMF, Phase 1), you may wonder if any violations occurred at the institutional or association level. Are the actions of the department consistent with the values purported by the institution? Are your values in conflict with those of the institution? If they are, what will you do?

With regard to steroid use, *law, policy, and governance* basic competencies (ACPA & NASPA, 2010) become more pronounced in the decision-making process. According to this group of competencies, "the internal and external special interest groups that influence policy makers at the department, institutional, local, state/province, and federal levels" (p. 20) must be identified. Athletic departments, in particular, have policymakers who are stakeholders in decisions about the behavior of athletes and coaches. Determining who should be consulted (DMF, Phase 1) is critical in this decision. What is your role here? Is there one particular department or interest group that absolutely must be contacted? You must be familiar with any guidelines/parameters that have been established by these bodies. What are the ramifications of known steroid use that would influence you in making a decision to report this incident to various individuals or bodies?

The major governing body for regulations in sports is the NCAA. The NCAA includes the use of anabolic substances as a violation of standards but leaves compliance, testing, and reporting procedures and policies up to individual institutions (NCAA, 2012). Your institutional compliance standards will inform your decision making. In your comprehensive scan of the options in Phase 2 of the DMF, you would also ask yourself what protocols are available for handling this type of situation. To whom should this violation be reported according to these protocols?

What other competencies might be relevant to this scenerio and your decision-making process?

But It's My Medicine

The new fall semester is about to start. You are working in the Office of Student Activities as the coordinator of new student orientation and first-year programs at Border State College in New Hampshire, in a small rural town less than three miles from the state of Maine.

The new students have arrived on campus, and your student orientation leaders are ready to help them become acclimated to their new environment. You assign Juanita, a rising junior and second-year orientation leader, to a group of 10 students. Juanita greets her group and, after some ice breakers, tells the new students about the college's rules and regulations, including those pertaining to drugs and alcohol. Both are prohibited by the college. Despite some grumbling, everyone seems to understand the policies.

On the second day, Juanita rallies her group and gets them started on their activities. As the group is about to go to lunch, John Ostein, a first-year student, approaches Juanita and tells her he needs to go back to his room to take his medicine. Juanita tells him he can go but to move quickly and come back to the group. John heads off to his residence hall room.

A half-hour has passed and John has not returned, so Juanita goes to find him. She enters his residence hall and knocks on his door. John opens the door and a cloud of marijuana smoke emanates from the room. She asks John what he is doing. He replies, "I am taking my medicine. I come from Maine and have a prescription for medicinal marijuana. I have an anxiety disorder and this calms me. It's legal." He shows Juanita his prescription card. Unsure of what to do, she tells John to finish up and come back to the group. Meanwhile, she comes directly to you and tells you what just happened.

 Using Phases 1–3 of the DMF, how would you respond? First consider the case as written, and then revisit your decisions in light of the different contexts described below.

Context Matters (Professional/Campus/Community)

1. What if your college is in a state that permits medicinal marijuana, but your residence halls are smoke-free?
2. What if it was an orientation leader who was smoking medicinal marijuana?
3. What if Juanita does not tell you about the incident? Instead, you find out about it via social media.

Competencies Matter

In incidents that violate campus, local, state, or federal law, you might quickly move through Phases 1 and 2. In such situations, your options for addressing the incident could be limited by laws or campus policies. However, campus policies, local, state, and federal laws can be conflicting. As noted in the *law, policy, and governance* competencies, student affairs professionals should not only be aware of the variations in laws that govern their campus and local community, but also be able to "describe the federal and state/province role in higher education" (ACPA & NASPA, 2010, p. 20). For example, laws regarding medicinal marijuana can vary. Currently, 18 states and the District of Columbia permit the use of medical marijuana by their residents, and 5 states accept prescriptions from other states where medicinal marijuana is legal (ProCon.org, 2012). However, at the federal level, marijuana is still classified as a Schedule 1 substance (i.e., high potential for dependency/addiction) under the Controlled Substances Act of 1970, and this classification was affirmed by the Supreme Court in *Gonzales v. Raich* (2005). The conflict between state and federal law could result in a person's legally possessing, producing, or distributing marijuana in a particular state while those same behaviors are simultaneously a federal offense. Medicinal marijuana is just one example of how variations in law can affect student affairs work.

Another issue in this case might be Juanita's response. In supervising Juanita and others, you might consider the ***human and organizational resources*** competency area skill to "demonstrate familiarity in basic tenets of supervision and possible application of these supervision techniques" (ACPA & NASPA, 2010, p. 16). What supervisory techniques do you use? How successful are they?

As a supervisor, you might wonder whether Juanita did the right thing or if she could have handled the situation differently. What if Juanita had not informed you of the incident? Would such inaction require a response from you? How might you use the ***ethical professional practice*** competency area and encourage her to learn how to "make referrals to more experienced professionals when appropriate" (ACPA & NASPA, 2010, p. 12)?

What other competencies might be relevant to this scenerio and your decision-making process?

Can I Help?

You have been hired by Extension University as an academic counselor. Extension is an online institution with one central (physical) campus of 5,000 students and 20,000 online students. Your job is to provide advising to all students (i.e., in person or via phone, e-mail, or university chat system). In most cases, students contact you about academics, but occasionally students talk with you about other issues.

One evening, you receive a message from Tyler. The online chat goes as follows:

Tyler1985: i need help.
You: What seems to be the problem?
Tyler1985: i can't no more
You: Can't what?
Tyler1985: all of it
You: What is your name?
Tyler1985: Tyler
You: Are you a student at Extension?
Tyler1985: yes
You: Are you a residential student or online student?
Tyler1985: i do school online
You: Where are you from?
Tyler1985: i'm home
You: Where is home?

Tyler1985: i don't want to say

You: Okay. Why are you feeling so down tonight?

Tyler1985: life just sux

You: What is not going well?

Tyler1985: everything

You: Are you alone?

Tyler1985: yes

You: Have you been drinking?

Tyler1985: yes. some

You: Are you thinking of harming yourself?

Tyler1985: i just want to b dead

You: Tyler, let me get you some help. Where are you? Is there someone I can call?

Tyler1985: no one can help me

You: Please let me get you some help.

Tyler1985: i just wanted to say goodbye to somebody

Tyler signs off.

 Using Phases 1–3 of the DMF, how would you respond? First consider the case as written, and then revisit your decisions in light of the different contexts described below.

CONTEXT MATTERS (PROFESSIONAL/CAMPUS/COMMUNITY)

1. What if Tyler told you that he would not harm himself?
2. What if Tyler told you that he had a gun and planned to use it?
3. What if Tyler had called you on the phone? Or stopped by your office?
4. What if you were unable to identify Tyler or his location?

COMPETENCIES MATTER

The thought of students inflicting self-harm can be very unsettling. In this case, the challenge of helping someone you suspect might commit suicide is compounded by the fact that your only connection is online. As you work your way through the DMF, your initial appraisal in Phase 1 is critical. What is the urgency of this problem and what is the threat level for Tyler? The American Psychiatric Association (2003) offers specific steps for the assessment of students who could harm themselves:

- Elicit the presence or absence of suicidal ideation.
- Elicit the presence or absence of a suicide plan.
- Assess the degree of suicidality, including suicidal intent and lethality of plan.
- Understand the relevance and limitations of suicide assessment scales. (paras. 49–56)

Despite these excellent suggestions, student affairs professionals must also consider whether they are adequately prepared to handle a student with suicidal ideation or other kinds of psychological distress. The ***advising and helping*** competency area offers some very clear suggestions for working with students who are experiencing emotional crises. First and foremost, you must "know and use referral sources (e.g., other offices, outside agencies, knowledge sources) and exhibit referral skills in seeking expert assistance" (ACPA & NASPA, 2010, p. 6). Referrals may be the best course of action, as mental health issues are sometimes outside the scope of our abilities.

A student might approach you with a problem but request that you not tell anyone else. Do you know when it is appropriate to break confidentiality? The ***advising and helping*** competency area suggests that we "maintain an appropriate degree of confidentiality that follows applicable legal and licensing requirements, facilitates the development of trusting relationships, and recognizes when confidentiality should be broken to protect the student or others" (ACPA & NASPA, 2010, p. 6). If a student reports the potential for physical harm to self or others, then you have a duty—and, in some instances, a legal obligation—to report what you know.

In your scan of options in Phase 2, you need to determine whether Extension has a protocol in place for managing students with suicidal ideation. If the school does, you should "initiate crises intervention responses and processes" as the ***advising and helping*** competency area suggests (ACPA & NASPA, 2010, p. 7). What if Extension does not have a protocol in place?

What other competencies might be relevant to this scenerio and your decision-making process?

Care for Maria

You are the coordinator of summer orientation programs at Amasa College, a small private college of 1,100 students. Amasa holds four two-day summer orientation programs that include an overnight component. All new students are required to attend and stay overnight in the residence halls. You have hired and trained an outstanding group of 16 orientation leaders. The orientation leaders work in teams and live on the floor with their first-year student groups. You have assigned Rebecca, a rising junior, and Maria, a rising sophomore, to the all-female floor of new students.

The first session is going great, and it is time for the residents to return to their halls for the evening. The night appears to be uneventful. In the morning, Rebecca comes to you and tells you that someone has written several derogatory remarks and racial comments about Maria, who identifies as Latina, on the women's bathroom mirror and toilet stalls. You check out the bathroom—the graffiti is very disturbing and filled with graphic language. You immediately call housekeeping and have it cleaned up.

You then go to check on Maria. You find her in her room, emotionally upset. She cannot understand why someone would do this. She thought she got along well with the students in her group. She asks to be left alone and does not want to face the new students. You allow her to be alone.

You pull together the group of new students and ask about the incident. No one admits having seen or heard anything. Later that day, one of the students comes to you to report that a group of students were hanging out in the hallway near the bathroom that evening. You approach these students, and they deny any involvement.

 Using Phases 1–3 of the DMF, how would you respond? First consider the case as written, and then revisit your decisions in light of the different contexts described below.

Context Matters (Professional/Campus/Community)

1. What if you discover that Maria wrote these things about herself?
2. What if you learn that a member of the custodial staff did this?
3. What if the incident goes viral on various forms of social media, and the Anti-Defamation League asks what the college has done to resolve the matter?

Competencies Matter

In this case, it is easy to see the need to be able to facilitate the learning and practice of social justice concepts, an intermediate skill in the *equity, diversity, and inclusion* competency area (ACPA & NASPA, 2010). Determining the desired immediate and long-term outcomes might be the most important task in Phase 1 of the DMF as you consider how to make this a significant learning experience in the lives of these new students. What do you hope students will learn from this incident about the need for social justice? What do you hope they will learn about how to handle such incidents in their own lives? What do you hope they will learn about themselves in relation to social justice?

In approaching and counseling Maria, it would be important for you to have intermediate-level competencies in ***advising and helping***, especially the ability to demonstrate culturally appropriate advising, helping, coaching, and counseling (ACPA & NASPA, 2010). Marini and Stebnicki (2009) recommended having an understanding of some of the unique cultural norms that might influence your approach to counseling or providing support. As one example, they noted that Latino/a students might place "high value on characteristics such as respect (*respeto*) when interacting with other people, especially professionals such as medical doctors, teachers, and psychologists" (Marini & Stebnicki, 2009, p. 234). On the basis of this assumption, you would try to be minimally intrusive in your questioning when you speak to Maria.

Further exploration of the needs and concerns of Latino/a students would assist you as you develop your ***advising and helping*** competencies (ACPA & NASPA, 2010). Rodriguez, Guido-DiBrito, Torres, & Talbot (2000) compiled useful information in "Latina College Students: Issues and Challenges for the 21st Century." In the article, they commented on how Latina students might experience stress resulting from family obligations and lack of support for their college attendance. They might also experience institutional marginalization at Anglo-influenced institutions, where they might feel "peripheral or separate from the mainstream university environment" (Rodriguez et al., 2000, p. 518). As you define the problem (DMF, Phase 1) and consider options for handling the situation (DMF, Phase 2) with Maria, you may want to ask yourself, "How knowledgeable am I about various cultures and how they might respond to my counseling and advising strategies?" What immediate steps should you take to be more sensitive to the needs of this student? In Phase 2 of the DMF, you are asked to solicit ideas from other staff members and supervisors about how to handle the situation. Other professionals on campus may be able to provide support and information about how to work with Maria with cultural sensitivity.

What other competencies might be relevant to this scenerio and your decision-making process?

Careful What You Say

The semester is going great. You are the complex coordinator of North Hall, your first professional position, at Friendly College. Friendly is a public institution in rural Nebraska with about 26,000 students; North Hall has 600 residents.

Recently, you were interviewed by the campus newspaper about some positive changes occurring in the building you oversee. The student reporter asks why you think things are going so well in your building, because this residence hall has had a reputation for excessive damage and constant partying. You say, "I think it is the right mix of people living in the building that has made the difference."

Early the next day, your supervisor calls. She asks whether you have seen the school newspaper and wants to know exactly what you said to the reporter. She tells you that the headline reads "The Jerks Are Out!" and you are quoted as saying that positive changes have occurred because "all the bad kids are gone." Former residents of North Hall are bashing you via every form of social media and calling the residence life office demanding that you be fired for calling them jerks. Your supervisor tells you that you will have to make a public apology for your remarks or there could be more serious consequences.

 Using Phases 1–3 of the DMF, how would you respond? First consider the case as written, and then revisit your decisions in light of the different contexts described below.

Context Matters (Professional/Campus/Community)

1. What if the students who were offended by your comments retaliate by vandalizing your office door?
2. What if you request a retraction from the campus newspaper editor and she agrees; however, when the next issue is distributed, the retraction is buried below some ads?
3. What if your supervisor does not want to hear your version of what occurred and systematically demotes you?

Competencies Matter

When information is distorted in a public arena, it is often difficult to repair the damage. Drawing on the basic *human and organizational resource* competency area skill to be able to "communicate with others using effective verbal and nonverbal strategies appropriate to the situation in both one-on-one and small group settings" (ACPA & NASPA, 2010, p. 16) will be vital to resolve this situation. Determining your desired outcome—one of the final steps in identifying the problem (DMF, Phase 1)—will help you establish the new message that you hope to convey. What message do you want to send? What new information needs to be presented and to whom should that information be conveyed? What venue would be appropriate to convey that information? Additionally, you may want to "determine if the message (verbal and written) communicated is congruent with the desired outcome for the intended recipient or audience," an intermediate-level skill in the ***human and organizational resource*** competency area (ACPA & NASPA, 2010, p. 17).

A situation such as this, in which the campus environment is negative in some specific way, may require you to apply some basic principles of community building, a skill in the ***leadership*** competency area (ACPA & NASPA, 2010). The *Handbook for Student Leadership Development* (Komives, Dugan, Owen, Slack, & Wagner, 2011) offers many useful ideas for developing student leaders who can influence the campus community. The handbook contains a list of the core values of the Social Change Model of Leadership Development offered by the National Clearinghouse for Leadership Programs. The individual values include consciousness of self, congruence, and commitment; group values include collaboration, common purpose, and controversy with civility; and community values include citizenship and change (Komives et al., 2011, p. 46). How might members of the newspaper staff or the residence life staff benefit from the dissemination of this information? Again—in keeping with the final steps in Phase 1 of the DMF (determining desired outcomes)—you might ask how this kind of intervention might help develop a more cohesive community on the campus as a whole.

What other competencies might be relevant to this scenerio and your decision-making process?

Conduct Unbecoming

You work in housing at Eastern University, a midsize, private, for-profit institution in the Eastern part of the United States. The university has made intentional efforts to recruit and retain veterans as students. The university has had much success recruiting veterans and active duty soldiers but has done little to structure support for these students once they arrive. Eastern is in the process of searching for a part-time veterans program coordinator, but that person has yet to be hired.

Yesterday, a resident in the campus apartment complex was documented for a violation of community standards. The incident report stated that he punched his roommate. As coordinator of the apartment complex, you will be looking into the case.

The resident, James, admitted that he restrained his roommate as a way to hold him accountable for unacceptable behavior. James explained that he has been best friends with his roommate, Brett, since junior high school. Brett was drunk and had been "cat calling" and harassing younger female residents. James thought Brett's behavior was disrespectful to women. James explained that he did not hurt Brett—he merely wanted to get his attention and show him that his conduct was unacceptable.

James could not get Brett to listen to him and pushed him as a way to get his attention. James went on to explain that he had just returned from deployment to Afghanistan. He said that this was how conflict was handled in his military unit. He also presented documentation from the V.A. hospital indicating that he was seeking treatment for posttraumatic stress disorder (PTSD).

 Using Phases 1–3 of the DMF, how would you respond? First consider the case as written, and then revisit your decisions in light of the different contexts described below.

Context Matters (Professional/Campus/Community)

1. What if your institution had a zero-tolerance policy for violence?
2. What if you worked at a for-profit institution that believed in giving students many chances before they are removed from housing or expelled (and tuition revenue lost)?
3. What if, after meeting with James, you considered him to be a threat to the community, but your supervisor disagreed?

Competencies Matter

As you work through a situation like this, a relevant competency area might be ***advising and helping***. One of the basic competencies is to "actively seek out opportunities to expand one's own knowledge and skills in helping students with specific concerns (e.g., suicidal students) as well as interfacing with specific populations within the college student environment (e.g., student veterans)" (ACPA & NASPA, 2010, p. 6). How knowledgeable are you about the concerns of student veterans?

In Phase 1 of the DMF (appraisal of the problem), which questions inspired you to consider your level of knowledge about veteran issues?

Because Eastern University is actively recruiting student veterans, the school may be offering training sessions or other professional development opportunities for faculty and staff. This would be an ideal and intentional effort by a university, but many institutions have recruited veterans with little thought to how to prepare professionals for effective practice. An incident like this one provides you with an opportunity to take responsibility for your own professional development. Ask yourself, "How might I increase my awareness, knowledge, and skills regarding working with this specific subpopulation?" To learn more about this population of students, consider attending conference sessions or a webinar on student veteran topics. If you do not have the funding for professional development, consider some of the free resources, such as the Veteran Friendly Toolkit (http://vetfriendlytoolkit.org) offered by the American Council on Education. This website offers a plethora of information about veteran benefits, student services, best practices, and resources for students. You might also expand your knowledge by reading the most recent research on veterans and active duty military. While new research is emerging regularly, you might consider the Association for the Study of Higher Education report *Veterans in Higher Education* (DiRamio & Jarvis, 2010) or the special issue of the *Journal of Student Affairs Research and Practice* (Manning, 2011) dedicated to student veterans.

You should be familiar with PTSD. Do you know the symptoms? Could you identify them when working with James or other students? Do you know that veterans might not be the only students who have PTSD? Any student who experiences a traumatic event can have PTSD. Are you prepared to support any student with PTSD? If not, seek resources to develop your knowledge and skills. In Phase 1 of the

DMF, you were asked, "Whom do you need to inform/consult as you move forward?" While there may not be a veteran coordinator on campus, who else might be an effective resource as you identify the problem and consider your options?

As you work with James and Brett, you should consider a variety of student development theories. Which theories seem most applicable to James and Brett? As you think about this question, you might draw on the *student learning and development* basic competency to "identify the limitations in applying existing theories and models to varying student demographic groups" (ACPA & NASPA, 2010, p. 26). We know very little about whether or how our current student development theories apply to student veterans. For instance, do our moral development theories apply to veterans who have undergone intense socialization into a military environment in which they are expected to abide by rules, policies, and rigid hierarchies? What other limitations might you find as you try to apply student development theory to practice with veterans and active duty military? You might have considered using Schlossberg's (1981) transition theory to work with James, who seems to be struggling with the transition from the military environment to school. Schlossberg's theory was not initially developed for veterans; however, DiRamio and Jarvis (2010) adapted it to be more relevant to student veterans.

As you work through this case and the Context Matters questions, you might wrestle with some basic *personal foundations* competencies. How do your personal beliefs and commitments shape your response to this case? How do your personal foundations influence the way you think about your response to James and Brett? As you ponder these questions, we hope you also consider how your personal foundations informed the way you identified the problem.

The author of this case talked about the ways her *personal foundations* intersected with a zero-tolerance policy on campus. As the case unfolded, she had to "identify key elements of [her] set of personal beliefs and commitments (e.g., values, morals, goals, desires, self-definitions), as well as the source of each (e.g., self, peers, family, or one or more larger communities)" (ACPA & NASPA, 2010, p. 24). In a zero-tolerance setting, students like James might not receive the support (e.g., advising, counseling, or other services) they need; in fact, they might be immediately removed from housing or campus. Would a situation like that shake your personal foundations?

What other competencies might be relevant to this scenerio and your decision-making process?

For the Record

You are a program coordinator in the office of enrollment management at a midsize private university located in a relatively liberal suburb of a large and diverse city. You supervise the front desk staff, many of whom are work-study employees. Because your office is so busy, student workers are expected to answer questions and help students with basic questions before referring them on to a staff member. To learn how to do this, they are required to attend a pre-employment training that covers the functions of your office. You also offer periodic in-service trainings about diversity. In fact, last week you had a guest presenter talk about the importance of respecting and affirming students from diverse backgrounds. The content was relatively superficial, but you hope to explore diversity topics more deeply in upcoming sessions.

It is a Tuesday in October and one of your student employees, Tara, is assisting a first-year student. The office procedure is that the student employee asks for a student ID number and pulls up the person's record so that it is on the computer monitor while assisting the student.

The student offers an ID number. The student name on the screen is Brenda Ashton, but Brenda introduces himself as Brian. He says the purpose of his visit is to change his name on official school records to Brian. Tara hesitates and then laughs. She says, "Seriously. What can I help you with today?" Brian responds that he identifies as a man and is about to begin the process of transitioning from female to male. As part of that process, he would like to change his name on his records so that class rosters, school ID, and other documents match his gender identity. He explains how his life would be much easier if faculty members would refer to him by his chosen name.

Tara says, "You can't just decide that you are a boy. Do you have any official documents showing that Brian is your legal name?" Exasperated, Brian leaves your office. Tara does not report this interaction to you. The next day, you receive a call from Trans Rights, a local activist organization. They explain that they have received a complaint from a transgender student about his treatment in your office.

Using Phases 1–3 of the DMF, how would you respond? First consider the case as written, and then revisit your decisions in light of the different contexts described below.

Context Matters (Professional/Campus/Community)

1. What if the student had medical documentation of sex reassignment surgery?
2. What if the student had a new driver's license showing "M" for male and the name Brian?
3. What if your institution was a women's college?

Competencies Matter

In this case, you could draw on one of the basic *equity, diversity, and inclusion* competencies to "demonstrate fair treatment to all individuals and change aspects of the environment that do not promote fair treatment" (ACPA & NASPA, 2010, p. 10). It could be that Brian, a transgender student, believes that the environment is not treating him fairly. The word *transgender* is an umbrella term. According to the American Psychological Association (2011), it includes people with a variety of gender identities, such as androgynous, transsexual, cross-dresser, drag queen, drag king, genderqueer, intersex, multigender, third gender, two-spirit, and gender-nonconforming. In a 2005 *New Directions for Student Services* monograph, Beemyn, Curtis, Davis, and Tubbs (2005) argued that colleges and universities have an obligation to provide simple procedures whereby students can change their names on official records. They noted that it is unfair to require students to provide medical or legal documentation to make these changes. Such requirements unduly burden students who are merely beginning a transition, cannot afford medical procedures, or live in states where legal changes are exceptionally difficult. Does your office have a policy that enables students to change their identity? If so, is it inclusive? Do staff members and student employees, like Tara, know the policy? To increase your knowledge regarding transgender issues, you might consider reading *The Lives of Transgender People* (Beemyn & Rankin, 2011).

In creating transgender-inclusive policies in your office, you might use an intermediate ***law, policy, and governance*** competency that suggests that professionals "appropriately consult with students or represent the student voice in departmental, divisional, and institutional policy development efforts" (ACPA & NASPA, 2010, p. 21). In Phase 1 of the DMF, you are asked with whom you would consult before you move forward. With whom did you decide to consult to identify the problem? Whom would you consult to consider your options? Are they the same people? As your office determines how to fairly serve transgender and gender-nonconforming students in the future, will you include transgender faculty, staff, students, and possibly community members? How might you locate these people?

As a supervisor, you may need to focus on your ***human and organizational resources*** competencies. One of the basic competencies is to "communicate with others using effective verbal and nonverbal strategies appropriate to the situation in both one-on-one and small group settings" (ACPA & NASPA, 2010, p. 16). Tara's response to Brian should remind you how important it is for everyone who interacts with students to have proficiency in this competency area. In Phase 1 of the DMF, you are asked to consider short- and long-term outcomes. What were yours? Did your long-term solutions involve more diversity training for staff? As a supervisor, you may need to consider in-service training for all employees about how to use culturally sensitive and inclusive verbal and nonverbal communication. Because your office had recently undergone diversity training, you might assess how effective that training was. How might you plan more effective in-service training in the future?

What other competencies might be relevant to this scenerio and your decision-making process?

Fraternities and Faith

You are the new assistant director of Greek life at Adams University, a large public university of 15,000 students in southern Florida. You are responsible for supervising the graduate interns, coordinating homecoming events, and chairing the Homecoming Planning Board (HPB). Homecoming is the most cherished tradition at the university. Because it is a large-scale event, the planning process usually lasts for several months and involves students, faculty, and staff. With nearly a quarter of the undergraduate student body involved in the Greek system, fraternity and sorority members are well represented on the HPB.

Two months before the event, one of your interns, Alisa Speyer, informs you that members of Alpha Epsilon Pi and Zeta Beta Tau—two historically predominantly Jewish Greek letter organizations—are seeking a formal meeting with members of the HPB. Unbeknownst to you, these organizations (as well as Hillel, a Jewish student organization) have tried for several years to get the HPB to change the dates of the homecoming skits—an elaborate variety show primarily sponsored by members of the Greek community—because the event conflicts with the Jewish Sabbath, which starts at sundown Friday and ends at sundown Saturday.

While the HPB wants to be inclusive and culturally sensitive, it has been reluctant to change the event schedule because the skits have traditionally been held the night before the homecoming game. In their eyes, the tradition of homecoming is what makes the skits special. For the HPB, this tradition trumps practically everything else. There was also a concern that making substantive changes to the schedule could adversely affect an event that usually raises several hundred thousand dollars for the university.

You invite the concerned students to the next HPB meeting and ask your graduate intern, Alisa, to take minutes. From the start of the meeting tempers flare, and the two sides cannot agree on a compromise. You decide to end the meeting, and you inform the students that the HPB will make a decision very quickly with regard to their request to change the schedule.

After the students leave, a faculty member makes the comment, "They just don't get it." Alisa, who is Jewish, is shocked by the statement and believes it to be anti-Semitic. She puts the direct quote in the meeting minutes and publishes them, without your review, on the homecoming website. This website is publicly accessible, and the comment goes viral. Public outrage ensues.

Using Phases 1–3 of the DMF, how would you respond? First consider the case as written, and then revisit your decisions in light of the different contexts described below.

Context Matters (Professional/Campus/Community)

1. What if Adams were a small private Catholic College?
2. What if a Jewish alumna threatened to withdraw her $2 million gift to Adams, earmarked for a new student center that is already under construction?
3. What if your Muslim student organization demanded a different change in the homecoming schedule, and the protest was supported by a national Islamic group?

Competencies Matter

As chair of the Homecoming Planning Board your tasks relate to the *advising and helping* competency to "strategically and simultaneously pursue multiple objectives in conversations with students" (ACPA & NASPA, 2010, p. 6). You simultaneously need to manage the HPB, ensure that homecoming events are inclusive and culturally sensitive, and manage conflicts among constituents with very different viewpoints. Respect for and inclusion of many voices in a decision-making process can be difficult to manage. Conflict in the workplace is inevitable, but in this case you are facing some extreme conditions. When tensions are high, proficiency in the following *human and organizational resources* competency is invaluable: "Describe the basic premises that underlie conflict in organizational and student life and the constructs utilized for facilitating conflict resolution in these settings" (ACPA & NASPA, 2010, p. 16). What constructs do you use in facilitating conflict resolution? One classic resource on conflict resolution is *The Eight Essential Steps to Conflict Resolution* (Weeks, 1992). Rather than seeing conflict as negative, Weeks suggested that conflict is an opportunity to build and strengthen relationships. Do you see this conflict as an opportunity to build and strengthen relationships? Another classic resource for conflict resolution is *Getting to Yes: Negotiating Agreement Without Giving In* (Fisher, Ury, & Patton, 2011). This volume offers specific strategies for finding mutually acceptable agreements for all parties involved in a conflict.

In your scan of the options during Phase 2, what role might tradition play in your decision? In broad terms, the ***history, philosophy, and values*** competency encourages professionals to be able to "articulate the historical contexts of institutional types and functional areas within higher education and student affairs" (ACPA & NASPA, 2010, p. 14). How do both the historical context and the Adams campus context factor into this case? Would your answer be different if the university were private or religiously affiliated?

In deciding if there are any secondary problems in this case (DMF, Phase 1), you might consider how you would address your intern's decision to post the unapproved minutes of the meeting. Should this be a priority, or should you wait until things have calmed down? How might you use the ***leadership*** competency to "explain the effect of decisions on diverse groups of people [and] other units" (ACPA & NASPA, 2010, p. 22) in your discussions with Alisa?

What other competencies might be relevant to this scenerio and your decision-making process?

Hand in the Welcome Box

Throughout the fall semester, Judy, a resident assistant from a low-income family, did more than her share of programs and was an amazing community developer. She was an excellent role model and peer counselor to her residents. They were so happy with her that they nominated her for the residence life recognition award.

As the end of the semester drew near, Judy began to worry about how she was going to afford books for the next semester. In the residence hall storage closet were leftover welcome boxes (free items from various local vendors) from fall opening. They included a variety of products. She came up with the idea of making holiday gift bags and selling them to residents for some extra money.

Judy reassembled all the soaps, notepads, wipe-boards, deodorants, and coffee samples from the welcome boxes into 50 holiday gift bags, and then set up a Facebook page to sell them. By Wednesday of finals week, she had sold all the bags and earned more than $200 toward her spring semester books.

As the resident director, you are Judy's supervisor. You did not become aware of the situation until another resident assistant told you what she had seen on Facebook. You go to the storage closet and find many items missing. The leftover welcome boxes were to be used for new residents moving into the hall during the spring semester.

 Using Phases 1–3 of the DMF, how would you respond? First consider the case as written, and then revisit your decisions in light of the different contexts described below.

Context Matters (Professional/Campus/Community)

1. What if Judy came from a wealthy family and was a business major with a strong entrepreneurial spirit?
2. What if the supplies had been thrown out and Judy retrieved them from the refuse bin?
3. What if Judy did not sell the items but instead donated them to a local homeless shelter?

Competencies Matter

After hearing the information provided by the other resident assistant and viewing the Facebook page, you may have come to a certain conclusion about this situation. However, as you learned more about Judy's background and her intentions, you may have come to a different understanding. Phase 1 of the DMF suggests that you gather as much information as possible to define the problem accurately. In the Context Matters section, you can see that changing the contextual framework of a scenario might make a difference in how you view the incident.

This incident provides the opportunity to "utilize theory-to-practice models to inform individual or unit practice," one of the intermediate *student learning and development* competencies (ACPA &

NASPA, 2010, p. 26). One possible explanation for Judy's behavior in this case lies in her stage of moral development. From the standpoint of Kohlberg (1976), she could be considered as functioning at Stage 2: Individualistic, Instrumental Morality. Judy recognizes her own interests (needs) in this situation and views her actions in an instrumental way. She has a financial need and does not think that what she is doing might not be fair to others. Rest (1979) might call this attitude "instrumental egoism and simple exchange" (p. 22), while Gilligan (1977) might see Judy's actions as coming from an orientation to individual survival.

In thinking about alternative contexts, you might realize that differences in moral reasoning challenge us to adapt our sanctions for the inappropriate behaviors we encounter in working with students. For example, should Judy simply be asked to sit down with you and discuss the implications for others of her choices and actions? Should she be asked to pay for the welcome box items? Should she be asked to acknowledge to others the inappropriateness of her behavior? Should she receive a stronger sanction that will have an impact on her paraprofessional role (e.g., a negative professional evaluation, removal from her position, or reduced responsibility)?

You answer these questions by determining the outcomes you hope to attain, as suggested by intermediate ***student learning and development*** competencies (ACPA & NASPA, 2010). Likewise, the determination of outcomes is an important step in Phase 1. Do you want Judy to learn from the event to enhance her moral development? Is the learning of other staff members an important outcome in this incident? Should anyone who has suffered a "loss" in the situation feel that some repayment has been made? Variations in context, especially in the background and motivations of the individual, play an enormous role in determining the learning outcomes, and the theoretical framework and constructs you use can affect how you view the student's attitudes and behaviors.

Other cognitive theories may provide additional insights in this case and offer new options for desired outcomes. Perry's theory of intellectual and ethical development (1968); Baxter Magolda's model of epistemological reflection (1992); the ways of knowing offered by Belenky, Clinchy, Goldberger, and Tarule (1986); and King and Kitchener's reflective judgment model (2002) approach Judy's actions in slightly different ways. These theories suggest that Judy's cognitive structures can be a focal point for determining desired outcomes and often recommend specific programs and procedures that provide role modeling for higher level thinking to promote cognitive development. To enhance Judy's cognitive development, you might consider pairing her with a mentor or offering her a group experience that challenges her thinking. What else might you do?

This case offers the opportunity to use your competencies in ***ethical professional practice***. You would certainly be asked to "assist students in ethical decision making" (ACPA & NASPA, 2010, p. 12) in the situation offered by this event and to "address and resolve lapses in ethical behavior among colleagues and students" (p. 12). Determining the extent of the ethical violation here might depend on your ***personal foundations*** basic competencies (ACPA & NASPA, 2010), which require you to identify your own beliefs, morals, and values. Does it matter to you whether Judy is from a low-income or a wealthy family, or whether she used the profits for personal gain or to benefit others? Is it more important to you that justice is served? These are just a few of the questions to ask yourself as you consider the many implications of this case.

What other competencies might be relevant to this scenerio and your decision-making process?

Honor Thy Father and Thy Mother

As an assistant director of the international student office at a medium-sized private institution on the West Coast, working with students from Asian countries has been your passion and your job. You and the director of the office manage all the administrative, academic, social, and emotional services for your international student population, which totals 125.

In recent weeks you have been particularly challenged by the needs of Sheng, an 18-year-old male student from China who is very depressed and homesick after nine weeks at your institution. Although many of your students experience homesickness, Sheng's level of depression is well beyond the norm. He is unable to sleep, not eating well, losing weight, and unable to focus on his studies. His roommate is rarely in the room and has not made an effort to befriend him. Despite your efforts to get him to socialize with others at events sponsored by the International Student Center, Sheng remains reclusive and uses the Internet as his main source of communication with others, mostly his family and friends at home.

In an effort to help Sheng, you recommend that he go to the counseling center. He refuses to go the center, because "Chinese culture teaches us that we should not speak about our problems with counselors," he says. "By going for counseling, I would be admitting to emotional problems. That would bring disgrace to my family." He adds that his parents have taught him that it is shameful to talk to strangers about personal issues and that you should only turn to family members and very close friends when you are in a crisis or need help. He has been able to share his problems with you and would like to continue receiving your support; however, you are not trained in mental health counseling and you believe he needs more professional help than you can give him.

Using Phases 1–3 of the DMF, how would you respond? First consider the case as written, and then revisit your decisions in light of the different contexts described below.

Context Matters (Professional/Campus/Community)

1. What if the student has invited you to communicate with his parents via the Internet?
2. What if the student's financial situation is such that he cannot afford to go home until next summer?
3. What if a professional issue has emerged in your office and you have been appointed to be the acting director of a different office?

Competencies Matter

As you proceed through the DMF in this case, you may find that determining the urgency of this situation (Phase 1) is the most important decision you will make. When a student is depressed, it is critical to establish the depth of the depression and determine whether there is a threat to self or others. One of the core competencies in the area of ***advising and helping*** is to be able to "identify patterns of behavior that signal mental health concerns" (ACPA & NASPA, 2010, p 6). The American Psychiatric Association (2003) offers guidelines for assessing suicidality of clients in emotional crisis. If you have any doubts or if you are not trained, consult with an appropriate counselor or mental health worker.

Another basic competency in this category is to "know and use referral sources" (ACPA & NASPA, 2010, p 6). You know that the campus counseling center can probably help Sheng, but he is not willing to go there. The counselors at the center might be able to suggest various approaches to engage this student. They might suggest that you attend the first session with him. Perhaps there is another international student who can speak to Sheng about his resistance and the value of going to the counseling center. Is there an orientation or group session for a specialized need or population (e.g., a group for students from China) that would be less threatening than individual counseling?

An intermediate *advising and helping* competency in this case would be the ability to "demonstrate culturally appropriate advising, helping, coaching, and counseling strategies" (ACPA & NASPA, 2010, p. 7). Huang (2012) identified issues related to the mental health of Asian American students, and Liu (2009) documented characteristics of Chinese international students that affect the nature of counseling services for these students. Specific cultural norms and nuances may come into play. As an example, Liu (2009) noted that traditional Confucian concepts have a strong influence on Chinese people; these concepts make them likely to restrain their emotions and discipline their behavior to achieve peace of mind. Liu also explained that in Chinese culture and medicine, the mind and body are thought to be integrated in such a way that a Chinese international student might seek help for a physical complaint—such as a sleeping or eating disturbance—rather than for psychological stress.

This kind of information would be most helpful for an advisor or counselor in developing a clear understanding of the core problem during Phase 1 of the DMF. The *advising and helping* competency goes hand-in-hand with the *equity, diversity, and inclusion* competency (ACPA & NASPA, 2010) that requires you to be able to interact with diverse individuals. Understanding Asian cultural values, hidden mental distress, social isolation and discrimination, body image and sexuality, academic achievement, and help-seeking issues is essential to effective counseling and advisement. Advisors and counselors also need to be aware of challenges that are common to all international students, such as language barriers, homesickness, and lack of social connectedness. What areas of understanding would be most useful to you at this point? What competencies would you need to enhance to work effectively with this population?

Another *advising and helping* competency (ACPA & NASPA, 2010) that applies to this case is maintaining confidentiality. All student development and counseling associations have confidentiality as a core value. The National Academic Advising Association (NACADA) stated that "advisors respect student confidentiality rights regarding personal information. Advisors practice with an understanding of the institution's interpretation of applicable laws such as the Family Educational Rights and Privacy Act" (NACADA, 2012). ACPA–College Student Educators International added that advisors and professionals must "inform students of the nature and/or limits of confidentiality. They will share information about the students only in accordance with institutional policies and applicable laws, when given their permission, or when required to prevent personal harm to themselves or others" (ACPA, 2006, p. 4).

What other competencies might be relevant to this scenerio and your decision-making process?

How Do I Work With Them?

You are a new professional at a private urban religiously affiliated institution; you are in your second year as a resident director. You have a staff of nine resident assistants and one graduate assistant. In January, an anonymous person sends you pictures of three of your resident assistants holding beer cans and drinking in their building during a party hosted by a student. All resident assistants signed contracts stating that they will not be around alcohol/drugs/paraphernalia and will not use these substances. These policies were reviewed in depth during all training sessions in which they participated.

You take the issue to your department leaders (director and assistant/ associate directors). After much discussion, they instruct you to terminate employment for the three resident assistants. You set up individual meetings with the resident assistants, hand them letters of termination, and give them a deadline to move out of the hall. You follow through with each of these steps. Again, all levels of leadership in your department have been involved in this decision and have told you how to handle it.

After you terminate the resident assistants, all three sets of parents come to campus to meet with the director and the vice president of student affairs. They deny the allegations and claim that the three students were holding cans for other students, not drinking themselves. They do not deny the involvement of their students in the party, but they believe that terminating them was too drastic a punishment. The parents give examples of other resident assistants who have been in similar disciplinary situations and have not been terminated but placed on probationary status.

After the students and their parents meet with the director and the vice president, the director calls you into his office and tells you to rescind your terminations of these three students. Now it looks as though you terminated them on your own, and the director found out and reinstated them. They return to your staff and to the same buildings; they will be under your supervision from February through May. How will you manage these students?

Using Phases 1–3 of the DMF, how would you respond? First consider the case as written, and then revisit your decisions in light of the different contexts described below.

Context Matters (Professional/Campus/Community)

1. What if you and the assistant director made the decision to terminate the three students, and the director was not involved?
2. What if the parents of only one resident assistant complained, and only that student is reinstated?
3. What if the rest of your resident assistants go on strike to protest the firing of their peers?

Competencies Matter

Decisions have to be made at three junctures in this case, and these decisions require competencies that help you deal with the complexity of the issues. The initial decision to fire the staff members is the first problem. However, as you proceed through the DMF, you encounter additional problems: the concerns of constituents (the parents) and the unintended consequence of the original plan (reversal of the termination, with you taking the fall for the decision).

In this case, you should be able to "describe appropriate hiring techniques and institutional hiring policies, procedures, and processes," an essential *human and organizational resource* competency in working to resolve these issues (ACPA & NASPA, 2010, p. 16). Your own knowledge of these policies would serve as a foundation for your understanding of the initial decision. Determining whether or not the staff member had a signed contract that delineated alcohol and substance policies for employees would be an important step in defining the problem (DMF, Phase 1). If the students did not have contracts, your institution might subscribe to the employment-at-will doctrine, which states that "in the United States, employees without a written employment contract generally can be fired for good cause, bad cause, or no cause at all: judicial exceptions to the rule seek to prevent wrongful terminations" (Muhl, 2001, p. 3). As you define the problem, key questions are "What is my role in this situation?" and "How much authority/responsibility do I have?" It is important to know the policies involved in terminating personnel in this situation.

Understanding "the basic tenets of personal and organizational risk and liability as they relate to one's work"—another *human resource and organizational resource* competency—would enhance your ability to formulate an argument regarding termination decisions (ACPA & NASPA, 2010, p. 16). Questions about the liability associated with the termination of employees without just cause, made in bad faith, or motivated by malice must be asked in states in which a "covenant of good faith" may be upheld (Muhl, 2001, p. 10). In this case, did your supervisors express concern over the possibility that just cause had not been established, resulting in their decision to reverse the termination decision to avoid lawsuits? Consistency in the enforcement of policies undergirds many decisions that may have legal ramifications. Phase 2 of the DMF suggests that you ask "How has this type of problem been handled in the past at this institution?" and "What protocols are available for handling this type of situation?" Do you believe that the parents' comments about past decisions for similar offenses should have any bearing on the reversal of the original decision to fire the staff members? Have hiring/firing policies been consistently enforced?

Knowledge of hiring policies and procedures in this case should be complemented by possession of the *leadership* competency to "articulate the logic used in making decisions to all interested parties" (ACPA & NASPA, 2010, p. 22). Your ability to articulate the bases of the decisions that were made and your role in these decisions would determine whether or not your desired outcomes would be achieved in this case.

Now that you will be supervising resident assistants whom you recently terminated, you will have to rebuild relationships. Your success may depend on your willingness and ability to "serve as a mentor for students," (ACPA & NASPA, 2010, p. 23) an intermediate *leadership* competency. Do you think you can be an effective supervisor and mentor to these resident assistants?

With whom can you share your concerns about how you were treated in this process? Do you feel unsupported? How can you rise above the behaviors of other staff members in a manner that reflects your values and does not interfere with your ability to work with these students in an effective way? The answers to these questions will reflect your basic competency in *ethical professional practice*, in that you are being called to "demonstrate an understanding of the role of beliefs and values in personal integrity and professional ethical practices" (ACPA & NASPA, 2010, p. 12).

What other competencies might be relevant to this scenerio and your decision-making process?

In Memoriam

You are the staff coordinator for the P.R.I.S.M. (Pride, Raising Awareness, Involvement, Support, and Mentoring) Center at Middletown State University (MSU). MSU is a public 4-year institution in the heart of the Midwest. The university has 12,000 undergraduate students and 4,000 graduate students. MSU is located in a predominately Baptist community with a population of more than 100,000. MSU considers itself a progressive and open-minded learning environment, but the surrounding community has taken issue with some of the programming on campus that is also available to community members, such as openly gay, lesbian, and bisexual presenters.

Michael Bret was a sophomore at MSU, an active member of the campus community, and an openly gay advocate for P.R.I.S.M. After more than 6 months of persistent mental and physical bullying by his roommate and other students, Michael committed suicide.

In his memory and in an effort to educate the campus community about peer bullying, you and several student members of P.R.I.S.M. decide to speak on the topic. You arrange a memorial program in one of the university's free speech zones, located in front of the student union. These zones can be used between 8:00 a.m. and 8:00 p.m. every day, although prior approval is required. The event is posted on P.R.I.S.M.'s social media sites and on the university's campuswide e-board, and flyers are distributed across campus.

Lighthouse, a campus organization that advocates a heterosexual lifestyle, has become aware of P.R.I.S.M.'s free speech zone event and chooses to hold its own event directly across the street. P.R.I.S.M members hand out flyers about peer bullying to people who approach the zone and on the sidewalk areas. Members of Lighthouse carry picket signs and flyers with negative messages about homosexuality. One Lighthouse flyer reads, "Students like Michael Bret should commit suicide for what they have done. All gays should kill themselves—it will make the world a better place."

The two groups begin yelling their messages to people who pass by, including faculty, staff, students, and other community members who support one or the other organization. Some people who are not involved in the free speech event begin to heckle the organizations. Because the free speech zones are not very large, some protesters are standing on the sidewalk, blocking the way of passers-by.

The president of the university is informed of the situation and authorizes campus security to shut down both events and clear the free speech zones. All flyers and picket signs are confiscated. Campus security officers inform organization members that they will be arrested if they do not disperse, but P.R.I.S.M. members are refusing to leave.

Using Phases 1–3 of the DMF, how would you respond? First consider the case as written, and then revisit your decisions in light of the different contexts described below.

Context Matters (Professional/Campus/Community)

1. What if MSU was a private university and students were not protesting in a university-designated free speech zone?
2. What if members of Lighthouse (including the roommate) were the very students who bullied Michael Bret?
3. What if this event was precipitated by a rash of LGBT suicides across the nation? The events, and the disturbing trend of youth suicide, have been the talk of local and national media.

Competencies Matter

As you work through this case, you may consider issues of fairness, justice, and equality. A basic *equity, diversity, and inclusion* competency to "recognize social systems and their influence on people of diverse backgrounds" (ACPA & NASPA, 2010, p. 10) might be especially relevant to this situation. Social systems and social institutions such as colleges and universities are often replete with heterosexism and homophobia. The bullying of Michael Bret and the Lighthouse flyers that read "All gays should kill themselves" are two obvious instances of LGBT bullying. However, for every instance of overt bullying, many covert acts go undocumented. A national study of more than 5,000 LGBT faculty, staff members, and students from colleges and universities across the United States found that bullying and harassment are common occurrences for LGBT people (Rankin, Weber, Blumenfeld, & Frazer, 2010). The study found that even LGBT students who do not experience specific acts of violence or verbal harassment can experience a campus climate as unwelcoming, invalidating, or unsupportive. Such environments can have a detrimental effect on the ability of campus community members to live and learn. In the most extreme cases, bullying and hostile environments can lead an LGBT person to suicidal ideation. Regardless of personal beliefs about LGBT issues, all student affairs professionals are expected to achieve minimal professional competencies in the area of *equity, diversity, and inclusion*. Similarly, in line with the basic *history, philosophy, and values* competency, you should be able to "demonstrate empathy and compassion for student needs" (ACPA & NASPA, 2010, p. 14). As you respond to this case and envision your future work at MSU, how can you show empathy and compassion for the needs of LGBT students?

Exhibiting competency with regard to *equity, diversity, and inclusion* requires a practitioner to move beyond personal levels of awareness and action to engage in system-level change. How might working for system-level change align with your short-term and long-term goals in Phase 1 of the DMF? Do your long-term goals include programmatic or policy changes?

MSU purports to be an open-minded learning environment that supports all students. Basic-level *equity, diversity, and inclusion* competency will enable you to "articulate a foundational understanding of social justice and the role of higher education, the institution, the department, the unit, and the individual in furthering its goals" (ACPA & NASPA, 2010, p. 10). As you propose programs to support LGBT students, promote civility, combat bullying, and prevent LGBT student suicide, how can you intentionally connect your proposals to MSU's progressive and open-minded goals?

Finally, the *law, policy, and governance* competency to "explain the concepts of risk management and liability reduction strategies" (ACPA & NASPA, 2010, p. 20) might also be relevant here. Do you understand the concepts of risk management and liability reduction? As you worked through the phases of the DMF, which questions, if any, got you thinking about risk management? Was student safety at the forefront of the decisions you and others made in this case? Given the grave consequences of bullying, did decision makers on campus consider the potential for bullying or violence at the P.R.I.S.M memorial service? What else could you have done before or during the event to protect both student safety and free speech?

What other competencies might be relevant to this scenerio and your decision-making process?

It's Not That Person!

You are a judicial officer at Little Patch College, a small private school in Kentucky. Recently, you adjudicated a case of domestic violence between Pat Hartford and Chris Booth. Pat and Chris are juniors who began their relationship when they met at orientation. From day one, they have been inseparable. However, their relationship has had problems from the start, including loud shouting matches. Public safety has been called more than once to address their behavior in the residence halls.

One Saturday evening, the yelling coming from Pat's residence hall room was louder than ever, and public safety felt compelled to key into the room to make sure everyone was safe. When they entered the room they found Chris on the bed with a bloody lip. They separated the couple. One officer took Chris into the hallway, while the other stayed with Pat. When the two students were asked how the bloody lip happened, Chris reported falling off the bed while Pat told the other officer that Chris banged into the door. Public safety alerted residence life, and a "no contact" order was issued. The local police were not called, but the incident was referred to your office for adjudication.

During the course of your disciplinary hearing, Chris discloses that Pat threw a punch that resulted in the bloody lip and that this was not the first time. Chris tells you that Pat has a really bad temper. Pat's story is different. Pat admits that they have frequent arguments but says it never gets physical. You decide to put Pat on probation and uphold the no contact order, which states that they may not have any contact with each other, including via phone, text, or social media.

It is midway through the year and they are in some of the same classes. You decide that you will not reassign their classes; however, you alert their teachers that they may not sit together or be assigned to the same group for any projects. Owing to confidentiality rules, you cannot explain the situation to the professors.

Toward the end of the semester, you are attending a college function and chatting with one of the couple's professors, Ellen Flowers. Professor Flowers tells you how surprised she was to learn about the problems between Pat and Chris, as they seemed like the perfect couple. She says that she heard about the altercation through the grapevine. She assumes Chris is the abuser and says, "It just goes to show you that you cannot judge a book by its cover. I have lost all respect for Chris, and the rest of the faculty feels the same. I hope Chris doesn't take any more of my classes. Chris should just transfer."

Using Phases 1–3 of the DMF, how would you respond? First consider the case as written, and then revisit your decisions in light of the different contexts described below.

Context Matters (Professional/Campus/Community)

1. What if the genders of Pat and Chris are not what you first assumed?

2. What if Pat and Chris are the same gender and Little Patch is a religiously affiliated institution that refuses to provide same-gender couples counseling?

3. What if Professor Flowers thinks she knows the truth about Chris and Pat and begins to tell others on campus (i.e., faculty, members of Chris and Pat's class, administrators)?

Competencies Matter

In your application of the DMF, one of the challenges in defining the problem in this case is to reconcile the differences in what the parties involved see as the problem related to partner violence. A second challenge is what to do about a secondary problem that has occurred in this case, namely the comments (and behavior) of Professor Flowers.

The theme of sexual violence pervades this case and is pivotal in determining the core problem. A national survey conducted in 2010 by the Centers for Disease Control and Prevention (CDC) found that an estimated one in four women and one in seven men have been the victim of severe physical violence by an intimate partner. The CDC defines intimate partner violence as "physical, sexual, or psychological harm by a current or former partner or spouse. This type of violence can occur among heterosexual or same-gender couples and does not require sexual intimacy" (CDC, n.d.b, para 1.). On the basis of these statistics, the CDC estimates that approximately 24 people a minute are victims of intimate partner violence. "Over the course of a year, that equals more than 12 million women and men" (CDC, n.d.a, para. 1.).

The secondary problem of Professor Flowers' behavior calls into play a competency in ***ethical professional practice*** that suggests that we "address and resolve lapses in ethical behavior among colleagues and students" (ACPA & NASPA, 2010, p. 12). How would you characterize Professor Flowers' comments in terms of their appropriateness or ethical nature? How can confidentiality, as required in the adjudication process, be maintained? How would you respond to Professor Flowers? What are the potential risks of breaking confidentiality in this case? How might the ***human and organizational resources*** competency to "explain the basic tenets of personal or organizational risk and liability as they relate to one's work" influence your actions (ACPA & NASPA, 2010, p. 16)? Providing students with a consistent level of confidentiality in disciplinary matters should be at the core of your work, even if this means that you are unable to address misinformation (e.g., Professor Flowers' assumption about who hit whom).

In some situations, campus disciplinary cases are also connected to the court system. How you manage the case, including confidentiality, could be subject to review by the courts. Adhering to your code of conduct, following your disciplinary process consistently, and providing a fair and impartial process are essential. As Kaplin and Lee (1995) noted, "Fair and accessible dispute resolution systems, besides being useful administrative tools in their own right, can also insulate institutions from lawsuits. Students who feel that their arguments or grievances will be fairly considered within the institution may forgo resorting to the courts" (p. 457).

As listed in the ***history, philosophy, and values*** competency area, you should be able to "describe the roles of both faculty and student affairs educators in the academy" (ACPA & NASPA, 2010, p. 14).

What is the history of relations between student affairs professionals and faculty at Little Patch? What is your role regarding interactions with faculty members such as Professor Flowers? As stated in the *Principles of Good Practice for Student Affairs*:

> Good student affairs practice initiates educational partnerships and develops structures that support collaboration. Partners for learning include students, faculty, academic administrators, staff, and others inside and outside the institution. Collaboration involves all aspects of the community in the development and implementation of institutional goals and reminds participants of their common commitment to students and their learning. Relationships forged across departments and divisions demonstrate a healthy institutional approach to learning by fostering inclusiveness, bringing multiple perspectives to bear on problems, and affirming shared educational values. (ACPA & NASPA, 1996, para. 18)

What actions might you take to enhance your relationship with Professor Flowers and other faculty members? How can you educate members of the campus community, including the faculty, about disciplinary matters and the need for confidentiality? Is this your role or responsibility (DMF, Phase 1)?

What other competencies might be relevant to this scenerio and your decision-making process?

I Won't Live With Him

It is summer term at Heights College, a small residential college of 1,100 students in Ohio. Heights College's motto is "Integrity in Everything We Learn and Do." You are the assistant to the director of residence life, working on fall housing assignments for transfer students. Using housing intent forms, you match two sophomore transfers, Scott Papel and Jared Dial, on the basis of common interests and lifestyles. Shortly after housing assignments have been mailed to the students, you receive a call from Scott. He reports that he tried to contact Jared, but the number was not working, so he searched for Jared's name on the Internet and found that Jared had been arrested for a drug charge (i.e., trafficking) while he was a student at his previous school. Scott demands that he be assigned a new roommate or he will withdraw. At this point, all the beds are filled and there is a waiting list of students who still need housing.

 Using Phases 1–3 of the DMF, how would you respond? First consider the case as written, and then revisit your decisions in light of the different contexts described below.

Context Matters (Professional/Campus/Community)

1. What if you learn that Jared did not reveal his drug arrest on his admission application?
2. What if Jared's legal case is still pending in the court?
3. What if Jared's uncle is a member of the Heights College Board of Trustees?
4. What if you learn that Scott is concerned because he is a recovering substance abuser?
5. What if Scott discovered Jared's criminal past after they had already moved in together?

Competencies Matter

A self-led study conducted at the University of Michigan in collaboration with the College Board found that roommate conflicts were among the top five reasons for a student withdrawing from an institution (Pleskac, Keeney, Merritt, Schmitt, & Oswald, 2011). Roommate matching is not an easy task, especially as many young people have never shared a room with another person. Add to this reality the power of the Internet and a generation of students who share highly personal information via social media, and the result is students who know intimate details about their roommates before they meet and who have little experience negotiating the realities of shared space.

As you identify the problem(s) in this case, what do you see as the core problem? As you read the initial case, do you think that Scott's demands are unreasonable? Do you change your mind as you read the fourth Context Matters question? In a *New York Times* article, Gaither and Conley (2012) wrote, "The dorm room is a student's only space to call his or her own. It needs to be a place of stability and comfort" (para. 3). How does this argument, from a non-student-affairs professional, relate to the notion of challenge and support (Sanford, 1966), especially when you consider that Scott might be a recovering substance abuser? How would you exhibit the *history, philosophy, and values* competency that asks that you "demonstrate empathy and compassion for student needs" (ACPA & NASPA, 2010, p. 14) when there is no way for you to provide Scott with his desired solution? In what ways could you apply the *advising and helping* competency to "mediate differences between or among individuals and groups" (ACPA & NASPA, 2010, p. 6)?

In Phase 1 you might need more information to establish a clear definition of the problem. The first step is to determine whether the information Scott shared with you about Jared is true. How might you confirm this information? What resources would you need to make this determination? *Advising and helping* competencies can be useful here. In particular, basic counseling skills of listening, rapport-building, reflecting, and "strategically and simultaneously pursu[ing] multiple objectives in conversations with students" would benefit you as you deal with this matter (ACPA & NASPA, 2010, p. 6). If you confirm the facts as true, what choices are available to you as you scan options during Phase 2? Whom might you consult for advice or suggestions? How would you decide whether to make a change? If there is a change, who stays and who goes? An *advising and helping* competency recommends that professionals "manage conflict" (ACPA & NASPA, 2010, p. 6). Can a conflict of this nature be managed through the use of previously existing protocols, such as roommate contracts?

What other competencies might be relevant to this scenerio and your decision-making process?

No Free Lunch

You are a new admissions counselor at a medium-sized private institution in a Mid-Atlantic state. You are new to the area and to the college, and are still trying to fit in. Like many institutions, your college needs to have full enrollment each year, and the competition for students is great. You and the other admissions staff members have a food service debit card that allows you to take people for meals in the food court/cafeteria. The purpose of this funding is to provide support for recruitment efforts. Staff members are encouraged to have meals with families, high school guidance counselors, and other people who can help them attract students to your campus. The budget for this effort is very generous, and the admissions staff rarely uses half of the budgeted amount.

One of the other new admissions counselors, Carmella Molinski, is a recent graduate of your college. She was a shining star at the college and is very well liked by the staff and faculty. You have noticed that she has been sitting with former student peers during lunch and that she is using her admissions debit card to buy their lunches. This has been going on for weeks, and the number of participants in Carmella's "free lunch program" seems to be on the increase.

 Using Phases 1–3 of the DMF, how would you respond? First consider the case as written, and then revisit your decisions in light of the different contexts described below.

Context Matters (Professional/Campus/Community)

1. What if you notice that the director of admissions is also very liberal in her use of the recruitment lunch benefit?
2. What if you discover that the budget has been depleted by April each year for the past 2 years, and recruitment lunches were curtailed at that time each year?
3. What if you tell the director of admissions about your concerns and you are told that this practice is simply a perk at your institution, despite the fact that other programs and services have seen major budget cuts?

Competencies Matter

One competency at the heart of this dilemma is to be able to "demonstrate effective stewardship and use of resources (i.e., financial, human, material)" (ACPA & NASPA, 2010 p. 16). This basic *human and organizational resource* competency suggests that staff members should not waste or squander the financial resources of the institution; clearly the staff member under criticism has violated the trust of those who have provided finances for the institution. Although you are not the person squandering the resources, you have recognized the error and want to move toward creating a more effective use of this budgetary item.

Deciding what to do about this dilemma requires some additional skills. As a new professional on this campus, you need to identify institutional mores and organizational structures—such as the networks, nature of power, and resource allocation processes—before you take any action in this situation. This would be one of the basic **leadership** competencies identified in the ACPA & NASPA (2010) document. Sometimes the use of resources may seem unethical or at least wasteful, but the nature of the institution has to be taken into account before you report such behavior. Without knowing the norms of the organization, you might report such an incident to the wrong person or not recognize that this behavior is rampant across campus. To whom would you report such behavior? An initial appraisal question (DMF, Phase 1) is to ask "Whom do you need to inform/consult as you move forward?" Is there a recommended reporting procedure for such practices? Is there someone you should *not* inform about this? Do other departments regularly use funds in this way? What might be the implications of reporting this behavior?

Sometimes you must resolve incongruence by employing competencies related to **ethical professional practice**, regardless of the ramifications (ACPA & NASPA, 2010). When incongruence exists among personal, institutional, and professional ethical standards, you have to try to resolve these discrepancies. Ask yourself whether this is one of those situations in which the incongruence is so great that you must find some resolution.

You try to consider all the available facts to arrive at a clear understanding of the problem (DMF, Phase 1). You might want to seek the advice of someone in your professional association who deals with ethics before approaching anyone on your campus. The *Statement of*

Ethical Principles and Standards (ACPA, 2006) offers clear direction in this case, stating that professionals should "recognize their fiduciary responsibility to the institution. They will ensure that funds for which they have oversight are expended following established procedures and in ways that optimize value, are accounted for properly, and contribute to the accomplishment of the institution's mission. They also will . . . [ensure that] equipment, facilities, personnel, and other resources are used to promote the welfare of the institution and students" (p. 5). How does this ethical statement influence your decision about how to act in this situation?

What other competencies might be relevant to this scenerio and your decision-making process?

No Partner Benefits for You

Southwestern University (SWU) is nestled in the foothills of a conservative city with a few million people. More than 30,000 students are enrolled at this 150-year-old institution, which boasts several professional schools. More than 80% of SWU students come from within the state, while 6% come from other countries. More than 10% of students live on campus in family-style apartments and traditional residential high rises. More than 500 children live on campus; thus, many parents stay at home and take care of their children during the day while their spouses attend school. These stay-at-home parents, who are on tight budgets, typically do not have transportation and are very interested in finding ways to visit the city and take their children on local outings. The dissatisfaction of these spouses is leading their partners to feel a lack of fulfillment with their schooling experience.

The issues of the on-campus spouses are brought to your attention in your role as the university's nontraditional student services director. You immediately begin to conduct research to learn what other institutions are doing to assist their spouse populations. You determine that providing a "spouse card" could be beneficial. Available for a small fee, a spouse card links a nonstudent spouse with an SWU student's identification number, making it possible for the spouse to check out library books, ride public transportation, and use the campus recreation center.

After you begin contacting organizations, you wonder if the spouse card is enough. In your mind, all couples should have access to the card. So you revise your plan. The new partner benefits card would be available to all partners, regardless of whether or not they live on campus or are legally married. You press forward and create partnerships with housing, off-campus services, campus recreation, and other entities. You are told by your immediate supervisor, Annie Davis, that you need to put your plans on hold until all the student affairs directors meet. Many of the directors who have been supportive in their conversations with you are now unsure whether they can support the partner benefits card.

During the directors' meeting, Bob Lankey, director of housing and residential living, says he likes the spouse card concept and believes that it could benefit SWU students; however, he finds the domestic partner part problematic. Lankey explains, "This just does not work for me and for what we want to do here at SWU. If you drop the domestic partner part, we can get going right away." He looks around the room and clears his throat. "Otherwise, getting this through could be a difficult struggle, and you could end up with nothing to show for it." The room goes silent. You break the silence by explaining that equality is important to you. You suggest that the partner benefit card could be a "lasting legacy of equality for the SWU campus." The meeting ends on a low note. None of the other directors want to oppose Lankey, who is a respected member of the student affairs team.

As you leave the meeting, Laura Boles, director of new student programs, asks if she can speak with you in private. You agree. Behind closed doors, Laura explains that although she does not know you very well, she loves your plan. She says the directors are afraid of going against Lankey. She also explains that things are difficult at SWU because there is a sort of "don't ask, don't tell" policy about sexual orientation.

In the next few moments, Laura "comes out" to you. She explains that she is not comfortable enough with her sexuality to declare it to the SWU staff for fear of what people might say. Laura asks you not to give up and to keep fighting for the partner card. Most important, she asks you to keep what she has revealed a secret. Laura says she will talk with some of the influential directors and see what she can do.

 Using Phases 1–3 of the DMF, how would you respond? First consider the case as written, and then revisit your decisions in light of the different contexts described below.

Context Matters (Professional/Campus/Community)

1. What if Laura never came out to you?
2. What if the pushback on your idea for a partner benefits card came from the president's office?
3. What if the student group for gay, lesbian, bisexual, and transgender issues heard about the resistance to the partner benefits card and their displeasure regarding the situation went viral?

Competencies Matter

Learning the culture of your institution and its idiosyncrasies is exceedingly valuable for new professionals. Birnbaum's *How Colleges Work: The Cybernetics of Academic Organization and Leadership* (1988) is a good source on how to understand the various types of operating cultures that exist in higher education. He wrote that institutions operate in four distinct ways—collegial, bureaucratic, political, and anarchical—that affect decisions and changes. He noted:

> Change in one part of the organization may affect other parts through a sequence of relationships, rather than directly. Responses to an administrative action may occur long after the action itself is taken. Small initial actions may have extremely large consequences, and because the interaction is nonlinear, the outcomes may not be predictable and are often quite different from those originally intended. (p. 52)

In addition to this classic text, a number of other resources provide insight into the complexities of institutional culture and climate (see, e.g., Kuh & Whitt, 1988; Tierney, 1990, 2008).

Sometimes what you believe is the right thing to do aligns with the cultural norms of your work environment; at other times it does not. The cultural context of your home institution can either help or hinder your decision-making process. One of the *personal foundations* competencies encourages student affairs professionals to "articulate an understanding of others' attitudes, values, beliefs, assumptions, biases, and identity as they affect one's work" (ACPA & NASPA, 2010, p. 24). In this case, can you articulate such an understanding or do you need to gather more data? In Phase 2 of the DMF, you identify any barriers that might prevent you from moving forward to a desired outcome. Similarly, an intermediate *leadership* competency suggests that practitioners be able to "identify potential obstacles or points of resistance when designing a change process" (ACPA & NASPA, 2010, p. 23). How might the culture of the school or the attitudes, beliefs, and values of the directors present obstacles to a partner benefits card?

What other competencies might be relevant to this scenerio and your decision-making process?

Not in My Backyard

Natural disasters are rare occurrences in your part of the country, so when you are faced with a warning about severe weather, you are not likely to respond with urgency. The academic year has ended and only a few students are on your campus. As a member of the admissions staff at a small New England college, you start your day with the usual admissions interviews, a tour, and reviews of applications. Late in the afternoon, you meet with 16 prospective transfer students for an informal presentation and a question and answer session. The meeting includes instruction on how to use online resources for information about college services, so you are gathering at a computer center on the third floor of the library. Only one clerical staff member is in the area where you are meeting. While you are presenting, one of the prospective students informs you that a friend texted him about a tornado warning in your area.

You are not aware of any campus warning system for such an unlikely event, and you have had no training for tornado emergencies. You assume that someone will warn you if there is an impending natural disaster and that you will be informed of any emergency plan that needs to be implemented. Two of the students say they are leaving the meeting so they can "beat the storm" and get on the road. You are not aware of any policy that would prohibit them from leaving the meeting. The two students leave. Other students begin talking about leaving as well. Two students check the National

Weather Service on their smartphones and confirm that a tornado warning has been issued. You look out the window and see a funnel cloud approaching.

 Using Phases 1–3 of the DMF, how would you respond? First consider the case as written, and then revisit your decisions in light of the different contexts described below.

CONTEXT MATTERS (PROFESSIONAL/CAMPUS/COMMUNITY)

1. What if one of the students at your meeting uses a wheelchair and there is a threat of electrical failures that will shut down the elevator?
2. What if a devastating tornado does occur and all staff members, students, and guests are asked to remain in building basements until the threat of other tornadoes is over and the roads are safe for travel?
3. What if the surrounding community is greatly damaged by the tornado and the city is unable to respond to the crisis and provide needed help, including police support?

COMPETENCIES MATTER

When a professional encounters a new situation for which there are few precedents, *leadership* competencies (ACPA & NASPA, 2010) come into play. One of the basic competencies in this category is to be able to "think critically and creatively, and imagine possibilities for solutions that do not currently exist or are not apparent" (p. 22). Even if such an event has never occurred, professionals can imagine the scenario and outcome on the basis of similar experiences.

In this case, a competent professional might decide that, although a tornado is unlikely, one should always err on the side of safety. Protocols and training in other areas can be useful. Later, this experience will provide you with an opportunity to influence your campus with regard to tornado warnings. Champagne (2007) offered suggestions about the elements of effective safety plans, which include prevention and response measures for natural crises. Response measures include establishing a crisis team, emergency preparedness, crisis management, policing, judicial measures, policy development, procedures, and counseling and emotional support. For example, are there enough trained campus security personnel to protect the campus against looting or intrusions after an event of this nature? Are campus counseling services adequate for a large-scale crisis?

Zdziarski, Dunkel, and Rollo (2007) published a comprehensive guide for campus crisis management that can be an excellent resource as you develop leadership skills in student affairs. The book includes a crisis matrix that provides a guide for conducting the initial appraisal of a crisis. The matrix aligns well with Phase 1 of the DMF—it provides information about how to determine the level of threat, affected groups, and immediate actions.

In reviewing these crisis response resources, it becomes apparent that you will need to have a basic-level *leadership* competency to "identify and then effectively consult with key stakeholders and those with diverse perspectives to make informed decisions" (ACPA & NASPA, 2010, p. 22). In this case, in the absence of a crisis team, whom should you contact during the initial appraisal (DMF, Phase 1)?

Perhaps the most important competency to be used and enhanced in this experience would be your ***personal foundations***. One intermediate-level personal foundation is to be able to "analyze personal experiences for potential deeper learning and growth, and engage with others in reflective discussions" (ACPA & NASPA, 2010, p. 25). Natural disasters, because of their unpredictable nature, give us a vast amount of knowledge about how our safety plans actually work and what is needed in the future. As you go through this case, what might you learn that can serve as a basis for future planning and protocols? What personal lessons might you glean from this scenario?

What other competencies might be relevant to this scenerio and your decision-making process?

Oh, My!

Mountain Community College (MCC) in Colorado is the largest community college in the state system. With more than 16,000 students, every office is overworked and understaffed. You joined MCC a year ago as a financial aid counselor.

You are one of four people who handle student financial aid needs. You enjoy the job and get along with everyone in the office. Because of the demand, everyone helps out. It is not uncommon for any member of the staff to go into another person's office to get materials, even if the person is not there. In fact, all staff members use the same computer password, so you can easily sign on to someone else's computer at any time.

Today is especially busy, and one of your co-workers is out sick, so it is just you and two colleagues: Tom Green, who has worked at MCC for only a few weeks, and Joan Williams, a long-time employee. It is lunchtime, but because the office is so busy, you tell Tom and Joan to go to lunch, and you will go after they return.

A student who has been working with Tom comes into the office to pick up a form. You ask the student to wait and go to Tom's office to find the form. It is nowhere on his desk. You assume that he had been working on it on his computer and had not printed it out yet.

Tom's computer is locked on safe mode. You enter the common password, and the computer becomes unlocked. You open a folder labeled "Forms" and click on one of the documents. When the document opens, it is not a form but a picture of a naked young girl. You quickly close the document and try another. Again, it is a picture of a naked young girl, clearly a minor. You see that this folder has more than 100 files.

Using Phases 1–3 of the DMF, how would you respond? First consider the case as written, and then revisit your decisions in light of the different contexts described below.

CONTEXT MATTERS (PROFESSIONAL/CAMPUS/COMMUNITY)

1. What if the nude photos on Tom's computer were of his wife or himself?
2. What if the pictures on Tom's computer were of various female students, but they were all fully clothed?
3. What if the campus has no policy on personal use of college computers?
4. What if MCC were a fundamentalist Christian college or a women's college?

COMPETENCIES MATTER

The *ethical professional practice* competency that we "ensure [that] those working in the unit or division adhere to identified ethical guidelines and appropriately resolve disparities" applies in this case (ACPA & NASPA, 2010, p. 13). As part of your initial appraisal (DMF, Phase 1), do you consider this situation an ethics violation, a legal matter, or both? What do you see as your level of responsibility to report what you discovered (DMF, Phase 2)? To whom should you report it?

During the course of your professional career, you will be required to master the ***ethical professional practice*** competency to "identify ethical issues in the course of one's job" (ACPA & NASPA, 2010, p. 12). When you discover an ethics violation in the course of your work, do you know what to do? How do you define something as unethical? We suggest that you refer to the general statements of ethical standards for the profession (e.g., ACPA, 2006) and those specifically designed for financial aid officers (National Association of Student Financial Aid Administrators [NASFAA], 1999). Another helpful resource is Fried's (2011) chapter about ethics in student affairs.

In addition to the ethical considerations in this case, legal considerations come into play. "Being able to describe how national constitutions and laws influence the rights that students, faculty, and staff have on public and private college campuses" is one of the ***law, policy, and governance*** basic competencies (ACPA & NASPA, 2010, p. 21). According to federal law (Sexual Exploitation and Other Abuse of Children, 2008, § 2252), to knowingly possess, manufacture, distribute, or access with intent to view child pornography is a federal crime. Federal law (Sexual Exploitation and Other Abuse of Children, 2008, § 2256) defines a minor as a person who is under the age of 18. According to the National Center for Missing and Exploited Children (n.d.), "In addition, all 50 states and the District of Columbia have laws criminalizing the possession, manufacture, and distribution of child pornography. As a result, a person who violates these laws may face federal and/or state charges" (para. 10). For more information on what constitutes child pornography and federal laws to protect children, go to the National Center for Missing and Exploited Children website (www.missingkids.org).

How does the ***law, policy, and governance*** competency to "explain when to consult with one's immediate supervisor and campus legal counsel about those matters that may have legal ramifications" (ACPA & NASPA, 2010, p. 20) fit into this situation? Is this situation beyond the scope of your position (DMF, Phase 1)? Do you know when it is appropriate to refer an issue or illegal behavior, and to whom? In Phase 2 of the DMF, you review protocols and precedent to conduct a comprehensive scan of the options. In this situation, how would you find information about protocols, policies, and precedent?

As you move through this case, you might ask yourself, "Do I know what is considered acceptable use of my college-owned work computer and Internet service?" Many colleges and universities have an acceptable use policy for college-owned computers and the institution's Internet access. To some extent, these policies are in place to prevent downloading or piracy of copyrighted material, which is illegal under the Digital Millennium Copyright Act of 1998. However, some institutions may have stricter codes that do not permit any personal use of a work computer, including online shopping, personal e-mails, or checking a Facebook account. Consider learning more about what is acceptable use of your college-owned computer and your institution's Internet access.

What other competencies might be relevant to this scenerio and your decision-making process?

Placing Pedro

You are working as an entry-level career counselor at Glance Community College in the Southwest part of the United States. Your primary responsibility is to help students find employment upon completion of their associate's degree. Many of the degree offerings at Glance are vocational, and the business community is quick to hire your students.

A student named Pedro Ramirez schedules a meeting with you to discuss his job search. Pedro is 28 years old and has been working evenings at a local restaurant to pay for his education. He is very well known at Glance and is involved in a variety of cocurricular activities. He has earned a 3.96 GPA and will graduate shortly with an associate's degree in paralegal studies.

You ask Pedro why he chose to study law and whether he has considered continuing his education. Pedro tells you that he wants to be an immigration attorney, but there is a problem: He is an undocumented immigrant. His family brought him to the United States when he was 2 years old. He does not have a green card or a visa. He hopes that if he works hard for a law firm, the attorneys might be able to help him with his immigration status.

 Using Phases 1–3 of the DMF, how would you respond? First consider the case as written, and then revisit your decisions in light of the different contexts described below.

Context Matters (Professional/Campus/Community)

1. What if you learn that Pedro did not arrive in the United States at age 2 but, rather, 5 years ago?
2. What if the state in which Glance Community College is located has strict immigration laws that require state employees to report undocumented individuals to the local authorities?
3. What if the president of Glance Community College is unaware of Pedro's status and has recommended that the college highlight Pedro as a success story in its print and online publications?

Competencies Matter

At the time this book was written, the issue of immigration was a political hot button and a source of dispute between political parties. The Supreme Court ruled on the controversial Arizona immigration law (SB 1070) in *Arizona et al. v. United States* (2012). Debate on the topic continues and the court's ruling has yet to be dissected. The issue will surely remain a focus of political debate for some time. While the debate continues, working with undocumented students will be a complicated issue. You may want to consider the ***law, policy, and governance*** competency to "explain when to consult with one's immediate supervisor and campus legal counsel about those matters that may have legal ramifications" (ACPA & NASPA, 2010, p. 20). This case, depending on the laws in your state and the stance your college has taken on undocumented students, may have legal implications. You may need to seek clarity from more seasoned professionals.

In the Context Matters section, we asked, "What if the state in which Glance Community College is located has strict immigration laws that require state employees to report undocumented individuals to the local authorities?" Because the college is a public institution, you are considered to be a state employee. How would you feel about such a reporting requirement? Would you willingly report Pedro, or would this be an ethical dilemma for you? One of the *ethical professional practice* competencies suggests that you be able to "identify and seek to resolve areas of incongruence . . . [among] personal, institutional, and professional ethical standards" (ACPA & NASPA, 2010, p. 12). If you disagreed with the policy, how would you proceed?

When faced with an ethical dilemma, how do you justify your chosen actions to others? Can you, as the *ethical professional practice* competency states, "articulate . . . [your] personal code of ethics for student affairs practice, which reflects the ethical statements of professional student affairs associations and their foundational ethical principles" (ACPA & NASPA, 2010, p. 12)? How familiar are you with the ethical statements and standards in the profession of student affairs? We suggest that you review them. Another helpful resource as you develop and articulate your personal code is Fried's (2011) chapter summarizing ethical standards and principles for the profession of student affairs.

What other competencies might be relevant to this scenerio and your decision-making process?

Power of the Press

It is 8:00 p.m. on a Wednesday night. You are the director of student judicial affairs and are working late. Your office is in a suite of offices for student affairs administrators and student organizations. The Interfraternity Council, Panhellenic Association, programming board, student government, and student newspaper all have offices near yours, and several of these groups are also working late.

You are in the middle of writing a report when the editor of the student newspaper knocks on your door. You have a great relationship with this student, George Redman, a senior communications major. He enters your office with a very worried look on his face and closes the door behind him.

George sits down in the chair next to your desk and clears his throat. "I'm not really asking for permission to do anything. I just need your advice. A student just came into the media room and told me that she wants to be interviewed and photographed for tomorrow's online edition. She says she was sexually assaulted by a member of the baseball team and she wants to tell her story to the campus. She says the guy is a predator and the campus needs to know everything about him. She says if we do not include this in our online newspaper, she is going to go to the local television stations. She said she was thinking about creating a web page, but she thinks it is important that the newspaper have the first word. I don't know what to do."

The student newspaper has a faculty advisor, but she is not available that evening. George says that some of the newspaper staff members think this is a great story that needs to be told. Others are very uncomfortable after listening to the details of the story. No one on the newspaper staff has spoken with the young man she is accusing.

George tells you the woman's name, and you immediately recognize it. You have been working with other university staff on this case. On the previous Friday night, the female student, a junior, met a member of the baseball team at a local bar. After having some drinks, they returned to the residence hall in which they both lived. After a session of heavy petting, the pair found themselves in the laundry room, where they proceeded to have sex. Sometime later, the young woman's roommate knocked on the resident assistant's door saying that her roommate was hysterical. She claimed to have been raped. The graduate resident director and campus safety and counseling staff were all contacted immediately and the proper protocols were followed. The incident was reported to all appropriate offices and the case was referred to you the next day.

You have interviewed all the parties involved and have begun scheduling the appropriate hearings. You met with the alleged victim, and she declined to file charges with the police. She said she wanted to have the university system decide the case. The young man has secured an attorney. You met with him and his attorney to review campus policies and university hearing procedures. Everything seemed to be proceeding as normally as possible.

Using Phases 1–3 of the DMF, how would you respond? First consider the case as written, and then revisit your decisions in light of the different contexts described below.

Context Matters (Professional/Campus/Community)

1. What if you did not have previous knowledge about the sexual assault?

2. What if your institution had recently been in the news for a number of highly publicized sexual assaults?

3. What if the editor did not share this information with you and you read it the next day in the online campus newspaper?

Competencies Matter

It is not uncommon to be caught between our desire to help the victim of a violent act and the legal issues that abound. In fact, an intermediate-level ***advising and helping*** competency requires us and our institutions to "provide advocacy services to survivors of interpersonal violence" (ACPA & NASPA, 2010, p. 7). Determining the most effective services and appropriate timing may be difficult. In cases of sexual assault, these challenges can be further complicated as you manage the needs of the alleged victim while simultaneously preserving the legal rights of the alleged perpetrator. How do you do both?

Some difficulties may arise in defining the problem (DMF, Phase 1) or knowing what options could lead to an effective resolution (DMF, Phase 2). Do you need to reflect on your own feelings about protecting the victim or the alleged perpetrator? Are you worried about the legal issues that could develop as a result of the article being published? How can you prioritize the issues so that the most important ones are addressed first? In what ways do you think the ***advising and helping*** competency of "strategically and simultaneously pursu[ing] multiple objectives in conversations with students" is applicable to this event (ACPA & NASPA, 2010, p. 6)?

One of your concerns might relate to how the female student in this case is reacting to sexual victimization. Fanflik (2007) noted that there exists "a complex combination of individual characteristics and external factors [that] influence how a woman will react to sexual victimization" (p. 5). Thus, "different psychological responses manifest different behavioral patterns or coping strategies for each survivor of sexual assault" (Fanflik, 2007, p. 5). For more information on different ways a victim of sexual violence might react, consider reading Fanflik's comprehensive report *Victim Responses to Sexual Assault: Counterintuitive or Simply Adaptive?*

In reflecting on Fanflik's statement that victims react differently to an act of sexual violence, how would you characterize the actions of the alleged victim in this case? Given your role as the judicial officer, what is your responsibility to her? Would contacting her outside the context of the judicial proceedings violate the ***law, policy, and governance*** competency that says you should not only be able to explain but also to work within the "parameters established by the internal governance system of one's institution as it relates to one's professional practice" (ACPA & NASPA, 2010, p. 21)? You should consider these and other issues as you ponder your role and responsibility in the situation (DMF, Phase 1).

In cases such as this one, the immediate needs of the victim often draw our attention. But what about the potential ramifications of the article on all parties involved, the judicial case, and the reputation of the institution? As you make your way through the case and move to Phase 3, what options could you consider that might either constrain the printing of the article or limit its impact? How might the ***law, policy, and governance*** competency to "describe how national constitutions and laws influence the rights that students, faculty, and staff have on public and private college campuses" shape your implementation plan (ACPA & NASPA, 2010, p. 20)? Smolla (2011) wrote, "The issues and conflicts that arise on our college and university campuses constantly present themselves in a constitutional dimension. Constitutional law, constitutional values, [and] constitutional traditions appear to either directly control or indirectly influence the ebb and flow of many campus decisions and events" (p. 2). The constitutional rights of students, faculty, and staff are different at public versus private colleges and universities. The two most significant areas of difference are the First and Fourteenth Amendment rights of an individual. According to Smolla (2011), "Private universities are not legally bound by the First Amendment's guarantee of freedom of speech, nor its prohibition on the establishment of religion; neither are they bound by the Fourteenth Amendment's Equal Protection Clause" (p. 8). What significance might these constitutional realities have in this case?

What other competencies might be relevant to this scenerio and your decision-making process?

Rolling Out the Welcome Mat

It is the end of October, and southern New England has been shaken by a blizzard. The devastation is immeasurable, and everything is at a standstill. Road travel is nearly impossible, with downed power lines, trees, and branches blocking major highways and side roads. Power is completely out in nearly 800,000 homes and commercial buildings, leaving many people without heat or water. The power outage has also created a shortage of gas stations with power to pump gas. Schools are closed. It is estimated that it will take as long as a week to get everything up and running.

Your small public mostly residential campus has full power because of its underground power line system. Rather than sending students home to unheated houses, the administration decided to keep the campus open and provide as many services as possible, including classes. Because it might be difficult for some faculty and staff members to get to the campus, students will be informed of closures and reduced services.

As assistant director of athletics and recreation, your primary role is to manage the athletic, recreation, and fitness facilities on campus. Your brand-new, state-of-the-art recreation and health facility is fully functional and is viewed as a wonderful resource for the college community. Your supervisor, who lives 20 miles away, will be unable to get to campus for the foreseeable future and has limited cell phone reception.

In the spirit of responding to crisis conditions, you enthusiastically open your center to the campus, allowing staff members to bring in family members without IDs to use the showers, take away bottled water, and generally take refuge in a warm building. However, you begin to encounter problems with this approach when you are asked to allow unattended children to stay in the facility while their parents work in other offices. People are using up the towel supply, and the bathrooms and shower areas are being left in unclean conditions. Additionally, you are very short-staffed because some staff members are unable to get to campus. The first day is one of endless decision making and stretching of the facility policies. You realize that you have reached the limit when a staff member asks if he can operate his slow cooker in your office during the day and residence life asks you to open the gym for pick-up games to alleviate pressures in the residence halls.

At midnight, you close the facility and decide to sleep on the couch in your office. The center typically opens at 6:00 a.m., and you are not sure who will show up for work in the morning. As you head to one of the bathrooms, you see that two commuting student staff members and their two friends are sleeping on mats in the yoga room. This final straw makes you ponder your strategy for the next day.

Using Phases 1–3 of the DMF, how would you respond? First consider the case as written, and then revisit your decisions in light of the different contexts described below.

Context Matters (Professional/Campus/Community)

1. What if some of the residence halls have lost power and you are asked to house 40 residents in your facility for the night?
2. What if the possibility exists of a power outage for the entire campus?
3. What if you are told to open the center for as many people as possible, including community members, but only a few staff members are available to supervise the facility?

Competencies Matter

As you go through the developmental phases of the DMF in this case, you may notice that you are challenged in your competencies and skills in a number of different areas. Phase 1, identification of the problem, asks you to appraise the urgency of the problem, decide what your role is, and identify desired short-term outcomes. These three aspects of the decision-making process will be critical in this situation.

Some professional competencies can serve you well in these decision-making tasks. In the area of *human and organizational resources,* you are asked to "describe campus protocols for responding to significant incidents and campus crises" (ACPA & NASPA, 2010, p. 16). What training have you received concerning emergency situations on your campus? What precedents exist for guiding your decisions and actions? If you do not have a well-defined campus safety plan, you may want to refer to *Creating and Maintaining a Safe College Campus* by Jackson and Terrell (2007) or *Campus Crisis Management: A Comprehensive Guide to Planning, Prevention, Response, and Recovery* by Zdziarski et al. (2007)—these volumes serve as source books for many safety programs. Zdziarski et al. (2007) offer suggestions specific to environmental and facilities crises, such as having students shelter in place until the crisis is over. They also describe the use of multiple communication vehicles during and after the crisis, such as a dedicated phone line, text messaging, and the Internet. With regard to *human and organizational resource* competencies at the intermediate level, you will have to be concerned about the effective development and management of facilities, policies, procedures, processes, human resources, and materials (ACPA & NASPA, 2010). Do you have enough staff to provide a safe environment for those who are being sheltered in your facility? How many policies will you have to override to allow nonmembers to use the facility? Do you have enough supplies (e.g., paper towels, mats, cleaning materials, soap) to service the community members in a clean and healthy way?

The use of your facility by people other than campus community members or for purposes beyond those stated in your mission statement may create some problems with regard to *law, policy, and governance* (ACPA & NASPA, 2010). This competency area requires you to be able to "explain the concepts of risk management and liability reduction strategies" (p. 20). Additionally, you may need to know when to "consult with . . . [your] immediate supervisor or campus legal counsel about matters that may have legal ramifications" (ACPA & NASPA, 2010, p. 20). What would happen if someone who was not part of your campus community was injured on your equipment? What if visitors are allowed to use the facility without officially signing in? What if the lack of adequate staffing results in an injury? These questions are pivotal for you as you go through the decision-making process. They mirror the questions in Phase 1 of the DMF. In particular, these questions target the idea that you have to consider some of the secondary problems associated with the initial problem. If, for example, you allow one or two of the staff members' children to use the facility for the afternoon, will you be liable if they use equipment without any supervision? What secondary problems might result in legal complications?

What other competencies might be relevant to this scenerio and your decision-making process?

Sally's Situation

Sally Thompson is a first-year student at Stony Creek College, a small liberal arts school in a suburb of Boston. Sally was diagnosed with Asperger's syndrome in high school. She disclosed her diagnosis to the admissions office and did not ask for any special accommodations. Since there was no request for accommodations, the admissions office did not share this information with any other office on campus.

During new student orientation, Sally met Rebecca Lane, also a soon-to-be first-year student at Stony Creek. After spending the day together, they decided to be roommates for the academic year. Sally did not tell Rebecca about her diagnosis. Rebecca thought Sally was merely shy and a little awkward.

About a month into fall semester, Sally began experiencing challenges with her transition to college. Although she was successful in the classroom, she was having difficulty making connections with other students. She began spending a great deal of time in her room, playing on the Internet, visiting social networking sites, and researching topics of interest (such as countries and their capitals).

Rebecca is uncomfortable with Sally's behavior and reluctant to take her to parties or invite friends back to their room. After Sally embarrasses Rebecca in front of a friend, Rebecca yells at her, accuses her of being "weird" and "immature," and says, "It's no wonder you don't have any friends."

You are the resident director of their residence hall. Rebecca approaches you and asks that you move Sally out of the room.

Meanwhile, Sally's parents have called you and shared her diagnosis. They told you that Sally needs structure and continuity in her environment to be successful. Her parents beg you to convince Rebecca to give it another try.

 Using Phases 1–3 of the DMF, how would you respond? First consider the case as written, and then revisit your decisions in light of the different contexts described below.

Context Matter (Professional/Campus/Community)

1. What if Sally did not have a documented disability? Would you handle this situation differently?
2. What if instead of Asperger's syndrome, Sally's diagnosis was bipolar disorder, and she has stopped taking her medication?
3. What if Rebecca and Sally lived in an off-campus apartment that was not under your jurisdiction? Rebecca asks for your help because she met you on campus once and found you to be helpful.

Competencies Matter

In a situation such as this, how do you "demonstrate fair treatment to all individuals and change aspects of the environment that do not promote fair treatment," as required in the *equity, diversity, and inclusion* competency (ACPA & NASPA, 2010, p. 10)? What would be fair to both Rebecca and Sally? As you scan for options and consider who might be negatively affected (DMF, Phase 2), issues of fairness should be at the forefront. To assess fairness, you might need to increase your knowledge about Asperger's syndrome. How much do you know about Asperger's and related autism spectrum disorders? Your answer to this question should prompt your consideration of another *equity, diversity, and inclusion* competency, which is to "interact with diverse individuals and implement programs, services, and activities that reflect an understanding and appreciation of cultural and human differences" (ACPA & NASPA, 2010, p.10). Given your present level of knowledge, can you effectively support Sally?

To learn basic information about autism spectrum disorders, including Asperger's, you can visit Autism Speaks (www.autismspeaks.org) or the Centers for Disease Control and Prevention (www.cdc.gov). Hurewitz and Berger (2008) suggested that students with autism spectrum disorders need more attention and cooperative planning with the host institution when they make the transition from high school to college, as "these students have been ill-prepared by their public high school to transition to college" (p. 109). Furthermore, "individuals with autism present a unique challenge to college disability services administrators, in that the students' needs often span areas that are not generally addressed or accommodated in a college setting" (Hurewitz & Berger, 2008, p. 114). Did you assume Stony Creek College had a disability services office? What if staff members in that office feel unprepared to deal with "nonacademic" issues like roommate conflicts?

One consideration in determining the desired outcome (DMF, Phase 1) would be to consider Sally's legal rights. How might the *law, policy, and governance* competency to "describe the federal and state/province role in higher education" be applicable in this case (ACPA & NASPA, 2010, p. 20)? How familiar are you with the Americans with Disabilities Act Restoration

Act of 2007 that further clarifies the Americans with Disabilities Act of 1990? Do you know the educational rights of persons protected under Section 504 of the Rehabilitation Act of 1973 and Section 504's relevant implementing regulations? For example:

> No qualified handicapped student shall, on the basis of handicap, be excluded from participation in, be denied the benefits of, or otherwise be subjected to discrimination under any academic, research, occupational training, housing, health insurance, counseling, financial aid, physical education, athletics, recreation, transportation, other extracurricular, or other postsecondary education aids, benefits, or services. (Nondiscrimination on the Basis of Handicap in Programs, 1999, § 84.43)

Specific to this instance, the nondiscrimination regulations also state:

> A recipient that provides housing to its nonhandicapped students shall provide comparable, convenient, and accessible housing to handicapped students at the same cost as to others. At the end of the transition period provided for in Subpart C, such housing shall be available in sufficient quantity and variety so that the scope of handicapped students' choice of living accommodations is, as a whole, comparable to that of non-handicapped students. (Nondiscrimination on the Basis of Handicap in Programs, 1999, § 84.45)

Do you think these subsections of the law apply in this case? Why or why not? Do you think Sally's condition supersedes Rebecca's right to live in an environment where she feels she can succeed?

What other competencies might be relevant to this scenerio and your decision-making process?

She Is Blitzed!

You are working as an academic advisor at Gregory University in Missouri. Gregory is a research university that specializes in engineering and computer science. The students are extremely tech savvy and are well known for their abilities relative to social media. Students at Gregory are electronically linked to each other more than at any other campus in the nation, something they are very proud of and that the university boasts about in its admissions publications.

It is Saturday night, and you are out having dinner with friends. Given that the university has more than 10,000 students, which is almost the entire population of the town, there is no place you can go without running into students. The restaurant/bar you are in is filled with students. Neither you nor your friends are loud or drinking much. In fact, you have had just one glass of wine.

You have to go to the restroom, but as you move to leave the table, your foot gets caught on one of your friend's purses, and you stumble a bit trying to move away from the table. A student sees this, assumes you are drunk, and tweets it to all his followers. The message is re-tweeted several times and then goes viral. You only become aware of it later in the evening when you get a text from a friend asking, "How hammered r u?" You check Twitter and see that it is everywhere.

 Using Phases 1–3 of the DMF, how would you respond? First consider the case as written, and then revisit your decisions in light of the different contexts described below.

Context Matters (Professional/Campus/Community)

1. What if you were, in fact, intoxicated?
2. What if your supervisor questions your ability to make smart choices about your lifestyle outside work?
3. What if Gregory University was a small faith-based institution with a long-standing prohibition of activities such as employees drinking in the presence of students?

Competencies Matter

When it comes to the intersection of your personal life with your professional life, you can be vulnerable when you are socializing in an environment where students are present. Intermediate-level *personal foundations* competencies call on us to be able to recognize the impact of this intersection and to develop plans to manage any related concerns (ACPA & NASPA, 2010). You might ask if there are other ways to find social outlets that are less risky. Would you be stepping out of the bounds of *ethical professional practice* by not identifying this situation as a potential ethical issue (ACPA & NASPA, 2010)? The *Statement of Ethical Principles and Standards* (ACPA, 2006) offers this guidance: "[Professionals should] avoid dual relationships with students where one individual serves in multiple roles that create conflicting responsibilities, role confusion, and unclear expectations (e.g., counselor/employer, supervisor/best friend, or faculty/sexual partner) that may involve incompatible roles and conflicting responsibilities" (p. 3). Does this competency apply to this situation?

In defining the problem during Phase 1 of the DMF, you might not see a problem at first. However, as the secondary problems emerge, you might ask yourself these two questions: "How will I overcome the inaccurate portrayal of myself on Twitter?" "What immediate steps do I have to take to keep this misinformation from spreading further or to forewarn my supervisor?" These questions reflect your awareness of the need to develop your *leadership* competencies, especially the ability to "serve as a mentor for students, new professionals, or those new to the organizational unit" (ACPA & NASPA, 2010, p. 23). How will you reduce the threat to your image as an effective mentor?

What other competencies might be relevant to this scenerio and your decision-making process?

Slandering the Survivor

Stanton Woodbrook is a senior athlete and very popular on campus at Frances Christian College (FCC). Stanton has been dating Laurie Pemple for more than a year. Stanton's lack of fidelity to Laurie has been the source of college gossip from the day they started dating; however, Laurie believes that she is Stanton's only true love and that he would never cheat on her.

You are working in the Women's Center at the college as a program coordinator and women's issues educator. Your focus is on advocacy for women's issues, but you also provide one-on-one counseling to women in crisis.

Meghan Roberts, a first-year student, comes to see you. During the meeting, she discloses that she was sexually assaulted by Stanton after a party while Laurie was home for the weekend. She does not know what to do. She says that Stanton has assaulted other first-year female students as well. Meghan tells you that she wants to press charges against Stanton. You help her through the process; eventually, Stanton is expelled from FCC.

Laurie does not believe the charges; she thinks Meghan is lying. The campus is divided on the issue—some people believe Stanton, while others believe Meghan. Laurie is convinced that Meghan fabricated the incident because Stanton rejected her advances and she wanted to get even. Laurie starts a social media campaign to have Stanton reinstated and names Meghan as the person who falsely accused him.

Some people (both FCC students and nonstudents) post derogatory comments (e.g., "liar," "slut") about Meghan.

The director of the Women's Center thinks something needs to be done and suggests that you publicly address the situation.

 Using Phases 1–3 of the DMF, how would you respond? First consider the case as written, and then revisit your decisions in light of the different contexts described below.

Context Matters (Professional/Campus/Community)

1. What if Meghan tells you that the slander is causing her so much stress that her grades are failing and she is going to transfer to another school?
2. What if Meghan had told you in the beginning that she did not want to press charges?
3. What if Stanton had been found not responsible and remained on campus?

Competencies Matter

As you work through this case, consider the ***advising and helping*** competency area. An important skill is to be able to "establish rapport with students, groups, colleagues, and others" (ACPA & NASPA, 2010, p. 6). In this case, developing rapport with Meghan would be critical. As a survivor of sexual assault, she may need more than just crisis counseling. In the

Context Matters section, we asked you to consider what you would do if Meghan tells you she is planning to transfer to another school because of the stress. You might want to use your helping skills to support her in making decisions that are good for her mental health and academic career. To address the social media slander, you might need to establish rapport with other students on campus.

This case involved an initial problem that, when solved, created a new set of problems. In Phase 3 of the DMF, you are asked to consider the unintended or unanticipated consequences of your decisions. Stanton's removal from campus triggered a new set of problems. What other unintended consequences might you want to consider?

As you navigate through this situation, from your first meeting with Meghan to the present, you might also find relevant the basic-level *law, policy, and governance* competency to "describe the evolving legal theories that define the student-institution relationship and how they affect professional practice" (ACPA & NASPA, 2010, p. 20). As a Women's Center employee, you are well aware of Title IX in general and, in particular, the *Dear Colleague Letter* from the U.S. Department of Education Office for Civil Rights (2011). The letter supplements the revised sexual harassment guidance document (U.S. Department of Education Office for Civil Rights, 2001) that summarizes the obligation higher education institutions have to take immediate action in response to sexual harassment and violence. The letter also reminds colleges and universities of their duty not just to react but to engage in prevention and education initiatives.

Is the social media campaign against Meghan creating a hostile campus environment for her and possibly for other women who have been sexually assaulted? In Phase 1, you were asked, "What individuals or groups—faculty, students, staff, etc.—are being or have been most affected by this problem?" How would you answer this question at the beginning of the case, when you are focused on the sexual assault? How would you answer the question once the social media campaign has begun?

Survivors of assault may get the message from the social media campaign that they will not be believed or supported if they come forward. Such messages are not only harmful for individual victims but can also contribute to a hostile environment for women. Campbell, Dworkin, and Cabral (2009) explained how self-blame and other mental health effects of sexual assault are intricately related to a variety of ecological factors. They point out that victims often interact with people and social institutions (e.g., college, university) that reinforce rape myths, blame the victim, and cause further emotional harm. In the *Dear Colleague Letter*, the U.S. Department of Education Office for Civil Rights (2011) addressed the potential for a hostile environment for victims:

> Schools should be aware that complaints of sexual harassment or violence may be followed by retaliation by the alleged perpetrator or his or her associates. For instance, friends of the alleged perpetrator may subject the complainant to name-calling and taunting. As part of their Title IX obligations, schools must have policies and procedures in place to protect against retaliatory harassment. (p. 16)

One of your responsibilities might be to determine whether FCC has policies and procedures to protect Meghan. If not, you might have an opportunity to use your leadership skills as you work with your supervisor and other campus stakeholders to craft policies that create a more supportive environment for assault victims. An intermediate-level *leadership* competency is to "create environments that encourage students to view themselves as having the potential to make meaningful contributions to their communities and be civically engaged in their communities" (ACPA & NASPA, 2010, p. 23). How might you educate FCC students about the ways their social media use is in direct contrast to how FCC would like them to make meaningful contributions to their campus community?

What other competencies might be relevant to this scenerio and your decision-making process?

Sophia's Picture

You are working for your college's service-learning center. It is winter break and you are chaperoning a group of students on a service trip to build houses in New Orleans. You have eight female and eight male students on your team. Everyone is getting along great and the group reports that they are finding the work rewarding.

On the fourth day, you are working with Sophia Milligan, a senior, who tells you that she plans to join the Peace Corps upon graduation. The team has run out of supplies, so you and Sophia take the college van to the local hardware store. During much of the ride, the conversation is rather dry and about the events that have transpired thus far. Sophia then begins to ask you questions about your personal life—whether you are dating anyone, what type of person you prefer to date. You brush off the questions and change the subject. She asks again, and you tell her that these are private questions and you prefer to not answer them. The remainder of the ride is very quiet.

Once back at the worksite, the focus is on the task at hand. You do, however, notice that on more than one occasion Sophia is physically closer to you than necessary. You continue to distance yourself from her, but she keeps coming closer. Finally, you switch jobs with another member of the team so you can work in a different room. At dinner that evening, you notice that Sophia waits until you pick your seat at the table and then sits next to you. You wonder if this is a coincidence or if you are being paranoid. You finish dinner early and tell the group that you are heading to bed.

In your room you receive a text message from Sophia asking if she may come to your room to speak with you. You respond that you are tired and that you will talk to her in the morning. You receive a second text from her stating that it is important. You respond by asking if it can wait until the morning. She sends a third text message, but this time it is a nude photo of her with a message saying, "Why wait until morning?"

 Using Phases 1–3 of the DMF, how would you respond? First consider the case as written, and then revisit your decisions in light of the different contexts described below.

Context Matters (Professional/Campus/Community)

1. What if another student in the group came to you and told you that Sophia had sent him a nude photo?
2. What if you were working at a religiously affiliated college?
3. What if Sophia is not a senior, but a 17-year-old, first-year student?

Competencies Matter

In identifying the problem (DMF, Phase 1), you are asked to conduct an initial appraisal of an incident. As you attempt to define the issue, you might consider whether it is an ethical or legal one. It is not uncommon for student affairs professionals to address unethical behavior, viola-tions of codes of conduct, and offenses of local, state, and federal law. If, during your identification of the problem, you view Sophia's behavior as a lapse in judgment relative to her ethical decision-making abilities, your assessment may fit with Humphrey, Janosik, and Creamer's (2004) view that "the breakdown of ethical behavior in higher education is seen often through the eyes of student affairs professionals in their day-to-day work" (p. 676). Ethical dilemmas can be tough issues for profes-sionals to address, as they can pose challenges to our value systems as well as to institutional standards of behavior. One of the ***ethical pro-fessional practice*** competencies suggests that we "address and resolve lapses in ethical behavior among colleagues and students" (ACPA & NASPA, 2010, p. 12). Similarly, *Principles of Good Practice in Student Affairs* calls for professionals to "help students develop coherent values and ethical standards" (ACPA & NASPA, 1996, para. 14). How might you most effectively address Sophia's behavior? Given your roles as both a professional staff member and target of the text, are you the best person to confront Sophia? Is this trip the appropriate time to have a discussion with Sophia about her values and ethics? The ***ethical profes-sional practice*** competencies also provide a variety of ways to think about your ethical behaviors. For instance, one of the competencies calls on professionals to "articulate and implement a personal protocol for ethical decision making" (ACPA & NASPA, 2010, p. 12). Do you have a personal protocol to follow in a situation like this one?

In some cases, unethical behaviors are also illegal. A number of ***law, policy, and governance*** competencies might be helpful as you work your way through Phase 2 of the DMF. For instance, you may need to be able to "describe the federal and state/province role in higher education" (ACPA & NASPA, 2010, p. 20) in regard to this incident. Sophia made an overt sexual gesture, but no state or federal laws bar sexting between adults. In the Context Matters section, we asked you to assume that Sophia was under 18 years of age. Many states have laws that prohibit sexting to or from minors, or forwarding pictures of minors. What implications might such laws have on your response to the case?

What other competencies might be relevant to this scenerio and your decision-making process?

The Dream Job

You made it! Almost. You are nearly finished with your graduate program in higher education and involved in your job search. You have sent your résumé to a dozen schools for positions in student activities, orientation, and first-year programs. Your dream job is to be coordinator of first-year programs at Best University. It is the perfect location for you, as it is close to your partner's place of employment and you hope to live together after you graduate.

Best calls and schedules a phone interview. You think the phone interview goes well. They tell you that they are just starting the process and have many more calls scheduled. They also indicate that they have a very strong pool of candidates, many with significant years of professional experience. They say that if you are selected for an on-campus interview, you will hear from them within two weeks.

Several weeks go by, and you do not hear from Best. You assume that they have filled the position. You are getting nervous about not having a job. You went on first and second interviews at St. Christopher College for a student activities position that has everything you want. However, it is a live-in position, and the school does not permit unmarried couples to live together on campus. St. Christopher offers you the job, and because nothing else seems to be the right match, you discuss it with your partner and decide that you do not have any other option. Although you are disappointed, you know that it will be a good professional experience, and you will make it work. St. Christopher is happy that you accepted and closes its search.

Two weeks after you accept the position at St. Christopher, Best calls to ask you to come to campus for an interview.

 Using Phases 1–3 of the DMF, how would you respond? First consider the case as written, and then revisit your decisions in light of the different contexts described below.

Context Matters (Professional/Campus/Community)

1. What if the position at Best pays $10,000 more?
2. What if Best contacts you just 2 days after you have verbally accepted the position at St. Christopher, but you have not received the written offer?
3. What if, after accepting the position at St. Christopher, you learn of a recent high-profile public scandal that occurred on their campus that challenges your core values?

Competencies Matter

Basic competencies in your *personal foundations* may be challenged as you make job decisions such as this one (ACPA & NASPA, 2010). To make complex career and life decisions, you will need to be able to identify key elements in your personal beliefs and commitments. In the case, you identified those elements and made the decision to accept the position. However, once your initial problem (unemployment) was resolved, a secondary problem occurred. How would you define this new problem? What new challenges do you face in your *personal foundations* as you deal with it?

The ethical consequences of the secondary problem are at the heart of this dilemma. Do you renege on a commitment to a job when a better opportunity comes your way? Multiple *ethical professional practice* competencies come into play in resolving this problem. At the basic level, you must be able to "articulate . . . [your] personal code of ethics for student affairs practice, which reflects the ethical statements of professional student affairs associations and their foundational ethical principles" (ACPA & NASPA, 2010, p. 12). Additional guidance can be found in the *Statement of Ethical Principles and Standards* (ACPA, 2006):

> Student affairs professionals will . . . adhere to ethical practices in securing positions: a) represent education and experiences accurately; b) respond to offers promptly; c) interview for positions only when serious about accepting an offer; d) accept only those positions they intend to assume; e) advise current employer and all institutions at which applications are pending immediately when they sign a contract; f) inform their employers before leaving a position within a reasonable amount of time as outlined by the institution and/or supervisor; and g) commit to position upon acceptance. (p. 2)

What does this mean for you in this particular situation? The answer depends on your ability to "explain how . . . [your] professional practice also aligns with . . . [your] personal code of ethics and ethical statements of professional student affairs associations" (ACPA &

NASPA, 2010, p. 12), which is an intermediate *ethical professional practice* competency.

One other competency might be important to you in this case. Being able to "describe appropriate hiring techniques and institutional hiring policies, procedures, and processes" (ACPA & NASPA, 2010, p. 16)—the most basic of the *human and organizational resources* competencies—would be helpful in your job search process. As you define the problem (DMF, Phase 1) of the conflicting job opportunities, you will have to gather information to formulate your final decision. What information is lacking? Would you handle this situation differently if St. Christopher had different policies?

What other competencies might be relevant to this scenerio and your decision-making process?

When It's Your Boss

You are in your first position out of graduate school, working as the coordinator of student engagement at Willow Woods College, a small liberal arts college in Montana. Your supervisor, Bob Scotch, the director of student engagement, has taken 12 students on a spring break trip outside the United States.

When they return, one of the students tells you that Bob was driving the rented van under the influence of alcohol. The student says, "We were all pretty drunk. It was one scary ride." You ask another student who went on the trip if this was the case. He confirms what the first student told you and provides you with a link to his blog, on which he chronicled all the events of the trip, complete with pictures of Bob drinking with the group.

Feeling confident that this had in fact happened, you approach Bob. He does not deny that he had imbibed a few glasses of wine but insists that he was not drunk. You believe that students' lives had been put in danger, and you are very worried about the fact that even in hindsight your supervisor believes he did nothing wrong.

 Using Phases 1–3 of the DMF, how would you respond? First consider the case as written, and then revisit your decisions in light of the different contexts described below.

Context Matters (Professional/Campus/Community)

1. What if a student is threatening to post the pictures of the incident via social media?
2. What if no other student verifies the incident?
3. What if this incident had occurred near the college rather than in a country where 18 is the legal drinking age?
4. What if a Willow Woods student had recently died in a drunk-driving accident on campus?

Competencies Matter

You would have to have an understanding of risk management and liability reduction strategies to appraise this situation (DMF, Phase 1). Understanding risk management and liability is one of the basic competencies in the *law, policy, and governance* area (ACPA & NASPA, 2010). Although your supervisor rejects the notion that he has endangered others, he clearly put students at risk. How would you challenge his lack of concern and make him aware of the potential dangers to student safety? What training might be needed for him and other administrators regarding issues of risk management? Does your institution have policies or guidelines that hold employees accountable for such risky behaviors? These are some of the questions you might ask yourself as you reflect on what you have learned.

One of the most difficult aspects of this case is trying to address lapses in ethical behavior by others. This is very difficult, as it might require you to confront your supervisor or possibly even report his behavior to a superior. Such competencies fall within the domain of *ethical professional practice* (ACPA & NASPA, 2010).

The *Standards of Professional Practice* (NASPA, 1990) support the notion that you need to confront behaviors that are not in line with legal codes of external communities. Professionals should "demonstrate concern for the legal, social codes and moral expectations of the communities in which they live and work" (NASPA, 1990, para. 7). A difficulty for you in this case might be to determine whether a legal or moral code was violated. If the answer is yes, how will you gather the evidence to support a confrontation or report the unethical behavior? What might happen if you do not report the incident? What might happen if you do?

What other competencies might be relevant to this scenerio and your decision-making process?

Your Career Begins Here

The mission of your small private college in one of the mid-Atlantic states is "Preparing for Careers That Count." Being a counselor in the Career Center seemed like the opportunity of a lifetime—you were excited at the idea of helping students on their paths to personal discovery and satisfaction. However, you were not prepared for the pressure to place students in jobs upon graduation. The recent economic downturn has created a difficult job market, and your college's claims of high placement rates are under scrutiny. Admissions personnel rely on high employment rates to bolster the image of the college. Additionally, the regional accreditation team will be coming next year and will be looking at outcomes assessment data.

One of your responsibilities is to document placement records for the college. During training, you are told to include part-time graduate studies and part-time nonprofessional work as full employment on employment records. Your supervisor is the assistant director of the center and is well respected in the division of student affairs. He has indicated that your performance appraisals are contingent on your success in finding job placements for graduating seniors. Thus, you may be asked to put in longer hours than you were told in the job interview. You are feeling uncomfortable about all of these circumstances and are unsure what to do, both personally and professionally.

Using Phases 1–3 of the DMF, how would you respond? First consider the case as written, and then revisit your decisions in light of the different contexts described below.

Context Matters (Professional/Campus/Community)

1. What if you find distinct definitions of the placement categories in the accreditation materials that state that part-time endeavors should not be included as full-time work?

2. What if you learn that the previous counselor was terminated because she did not meet performance/productivity standards?

3. What if you discover that previous placement data were enhanced?

Competencies Matter

As an entry-level professional, it is understandable that you might question some actions at your new workplace, especially those that conflict with your personal values. One basic competency that applies in this case is the ***personal foundations*** competency of identifying work responsibilities and one's own strengths and limitations (ACPA & NASPA, 2010). Perhaps you do not have a complete understanding of the reporting process on this campus, or you do not have access to a comprehensive set of statistics. You might not be fully aware of all aspects of the process. In Phase 1 of the DMF, you are asked to define the problem as clearly as you can by asking yourself such questions as

"What is my role in this problem?" and "How much power and responsibility do I have?" You might want to find out if others are worried about the overreporting and, if so, how they are handling their involvement. At the same time, you may have to determine whether it is your role or responsibility to review office procedures.

Another ***personal foundations*** competency that might come up in this case is your ability to "identify sources of dissonance and fulfillment in … [your] life and take appropriate steps in response" (ACPA & NASPA, 2010, p. 24). You have been told that this position will require more hours than what was stated when you were hired, and you have concerns about the impact this might have on your quality of life. What steps will you take, if any, to maintain your own work-life balance?

In keeping with the professional competency of ***assessment, evaluation, and research*** (ACPA & NASPA, 2010), you will have to "facilitate *appropriate* [emphasis added] data collection for system/department-wide assessment and evaluation efforts" (p. 8). In this case, you might question the existing collection methods to ensure that the assessment is appropriate. Asking a supervisor for professional guidelines about this type of data collection could be helpful. In Phase 1 of the DMF, for example, you are guided to gather information to define the problem before taking action.

Your behavior in this situation might "model the principles of the profession and communicate the expectation of the same from colleagues and supervisees," one of the competencies in the ***history, philosophy, and values*** area (ACPA & NASPA, 2010, p. 14). Although it can be hard for a new professional to do so, it behooves you to act in a manner that reflects the values of the profession. Can you think of any indirect ways to question others about the reporting methods that will further the goal of honorability in reporting? For example, might copies of reporting guidelines be distributed or posted in some manner that will call attention to the actual reporting requirements?

What other competencies might be relevant to this scenerio and your decision-making process?

REFERENCES

American College Personnel Association (ACPA). (2006). *Statement of ethical principles and standards.* Retrieved from http://www.myacpa.org/au/documents/Ethical_Principles_Standards.pdf

American College Personnel Association (ACPA) and National Association of Student Personnel Administrators (NASPA). (1996). *Principles of good practice for student affairs.* Retrieved from http://www.naspa.org/career/goodprac.cfm

American College Personnel Association (ACPA) and National Association of Student Personnel Administrators (NASPA). (2010). *Professional competency areas for student affairs practitioners.* Retrieved from http://www.naspa.org/programs/prodev/Professional_Competencies.pdf

American Psychiatric Association. (2003). *Practice guidelines for the assessment and treatment of patients with suicidal behaviors.* Retrieved from http://psychiatryonline.org/content.aspx?bookid=28&sectionid=1673332#56135

American Psychological Association. (2011). *Answers to your questions: About transgender people, gender identity, and gender expression.* Retrieved from http://www.apa.org/topics/sexuality/transgender.pdf

Arizona et al. v. United States, 132 S. Ct. 2492 (2012).

Baxter Magolda, M. B. (1992). *Knowing and reasoning in college: Gender-related patterns in students' intellectual development.* San Francisco, CA: Jossey-Bass.

Beemyn, B., Curtis, B., Davis, M., & Tubbs, N. J. (2005). Transgender issues on college campuses. In R. Sanlo (Ed.), *Gender identity and sexual orientation: Research. Policy. and personal perspectives* (New directions for student services, No. 111, pp. 49–60). San Francisco, CA: Jossey-Bass.

Beemyn, G., & Rankin, S. (2011). *The lives of transgender people.* New York, NY: Columbia University Press.

Belenky, M. F., Clinchy, B. M., Goldberger, N. R., & Tarule, J. M. (1986). *Women's way of knowing: The development of self, voice, and mind.* New York, NY: Basic.

Birnbaum, R. (1988). *How colleges work: The cybernetics of academic organizations and leadership.* San Francisco, CA: Jossey-Bass.

Campbell, R., Dworkin, E., & Cabral, G. (2009). An ecological model of the impact of sexual assault on women's mental health. *Trauma, Violence, and Abuse, 10*(3), *225–246.*

Centers for Disease Control and Prevention (CDC). (n.d.a). *New data on domestic and sexual violence.* Retrieved from http://www.cdc.gov/Features/NISVS

Centers for Disease Control and Prevention (CDC). (n.d.b). *Intimate partner violence.* Retrieved from http://www.cdc.gov/ViolencePrevention/intimatepartnerviolence/index.html

Champagne, D. (2007). Elements of a comprehensive safety plan. In J. F. Jackson & M. Terrell (Eds.), *Creating and maintaining safe college campuses: A sourcebook for evaluating and enhancing safety programs* (pp. 261–273). Sterling, VA: Stylus.

Digital Millennium Copyright Act of 1998, Pub. L. No. 105-304, 112 Stat. 2860 (1998).

DiRamio, D., & Jarvis, K. (2010). *Veterans in higher education: When Johnny and Jane come marching to campus* (ASHE Higher Education Report, Vol. 37, No. 3). Hoboken, NJ: Wiley.

Ellison, N. B., Hancock, J. T., & Toma, C. L. (2012). Profile as promise: A framework for conceptualizing veracity in online dating self-presentations. *New Media and Society, 14*(1), 45–62. doi: 10.1177/1461444811410395

Fanflik, P. L. (2007). *Victim responses to sexual assault: Counterintuitive or simply adaptive?* Retrieved from http://www.ndaa.org/pdf/ pub_victim_responses_sexual_assault.pdf

Fisher, R., Ury, W., & Patton, B. (2011). *Getting to yes: Negotiating agreement without giving in* (3rd ed.). New York, NY: Penguin.

Fried, J. (2011). Ethical standards and principles. In J. H. Schuh, S. R. Jones, & S. R. Harper (Eds.), *Student services: A handbook for the profession* (5th ed., pp. 96–119). San Francisco, CA: Jossey-Bass.

Gaither, J., & Conley, D. (2012, April 23). Should college freshmen choose their own roommates? *New York Times Upfront*, p. 22.

Gilligan, C. (1977). In a different voice: Women's conception of self and morality. *Harvard Educational Review, 47*, 481–517.

Gonzales v. Raich, 545 U.S. 1 (2005).

Huang, K. (2012). Asian American mental health on campus. In D. Ching & A. Agbayani (Eds.), *Asian Americans and Pacific Islanders in higher education: Research and perspectives on identity, leadership, and success* (pp. 231–245). Washington, DC: National Association of Student Personnel Administrators.

Humphrey, E., Janosik, S. M., & Creamer, D. G. (2004). The role of principles, characters, and professional values in ethical decision-making. *NASPA Journal, 41*(3), 675–692.

Hurewitz, F., & Berger, P. E. (2008). Preparing students with autism for college, and preparing colleges for students with autism. *Speaker's Journal, 8*(11), 109–117.

Jackson, J. F., & Terrell, M. (Eds.). (2007). *Creating and maintaining safe college campuses: A sourcebook for evaluating and enhancing safety programs.* Sterling, VA: Stylus.

Kacprzyk, J., Federizzi, M., & Nurmi, H. (1992). Group decision making and consensus under fuzzy preferences and fuzzy majority. *Fuzzy Sets and Systems, 49*(1), 21–31.

Kaplin, W. A., & Lee, B. A. (1995). *The law of higher education* (3rd ed.). San Francisco, CA: Jossey-Bass.

King, P. M. & Kitchener, K. S. (2002). The reflective judgment model: Twenty years of research on epistemic cognition. In B. K. Hofer & P. R. Pintrich (Eds.), *Personal epistemology: The psychology of beliefs about knowledge and knowing,* (pp. 37–61). Mahway, NJ: Lawrence Erlbaum.

Kohlberg, L. (1976). Moral stages and moralization: The cognitive-developmental approach. In T. Lickona (Ed.), *Moral development and behavior: Theory, research, and social issues* (pp. 31–53). New York, NY: Holt, Rinehart and Winston.

Komives, S. R., Dugan, J. P., Owen, J. E., Slack, C., & Wagner, W. (2011). *The handbook for student leadership development* (2nd ed.). San Francisco, CA: Jossey-Bass.

Kuh, G. D., & Whitt, E. J. (1988). *The invisible tapestry: Culture in American colleges and universities* (ASHE-ERIC Higher Education Reports, Vol. 17, No. 1). Washington, DC: Association for the Study of Higher Education.

Liu, M. (2009). Addressing the mental health problems of Chinese international college students in the United States. *Advances in Social Work, 10*(1), 69–86.

Manning, K. (Ed.). (2011). *Journal of Student Affairs Research and Practice, 48*(3).

Marini, I., & Stebnicki, M. (Eds.). (2009). *A professional counselor's desk reference.* New York, NY: Springer.

Muhl, C. J. (2001). The employment-at-will doctrine: Three major exceptions. *Monthly Labor Review, 124*(1), 3–11.

National Academic Advising Association (NACADA). (2012). *Statement of core values of academic advising.* Retrieved from http://.www.nacada. ksu.edu/clearinghouse/advisingissues/core-values.htm

National Association of Academic Advisors for Athletics (N4A). (2012). *Code of ethics.* Retrieved from http://grfx.cstv.com/ photos/schools/nacda/sports/nfoura/auto_pdf/2011-12/misc_ non_event/codeofethics.pdf

National Association of Student Financial Aid Administrators (NASFAA). (1999). *NASFAA's statement of ethical principles and code of conduct for institutional financial aid professionals.* Retrieved from http://www.nasfaa.org/mkt/about/Statement_of_Ethical_ Principles.aspx

National Association of Student Personnel Administrators (NASPA). (1990). *Standards of professional practice.* Retrieved from http://www.naspa.org/about/standards.cfm

National Center for Missing and Exploited Children. (n.d.). *What is child pornography.* Retrieved from http://www.missingkids.com/missingkids/servlet/PageServlet?LanguageCountry=en_US&PageId=1504

National Collegiate Athletic Association (NCAA). (2012). *Rules compliance: Enforcement.* Retrieved from http://www.ncaa/wps/wcm/connect/public/ncaa/enforcment/index.html

Nondiscrimination on the Basis of Handicap in Programs or Activities Receiving Federal Financial Assistance, 45 C.F.R §§ 84.43–84.45 (1999).

Perry, W. G., Jr. (1968). *Forms of intellectual and ethical development in the college years: A scheme.* New York, NY: Holt, Rinehart and Winston.

Pleskac, T. J., Keeney, J., Merritt, S. M., Schmitt, N., & Oswald, F. L. (2011). A detection model of college withdrawal. *Organizational Behavior and Human Decision Processes, 115*(1), 85–98.

ProCon.org. (2012, December 6). *18 legal medical marijuana states and DC: Laws, fees, and possession limits.* Retrieved from http://medicalmarijuana.procon.org/view.resource.php?resourceID=000881

Pujazon-Zazik, M. A., Manasse, S. M., & Orrell-Valente, J. K. (2012). Adolescents' self-presentation on a teen dating web site: A risk-content analysis. *Journal of Adolescent Health, 50*(5), 517–520. doi: 10.1016/jadohealth.2011.11.015

Rankin, S., Weber, G., Blumenfeld, W., & Frazer, S. (2010). *The state of higher education for lesbian, gay, bisexual and transgender people.* Charlotte, NC: Campus Pride.

Renn, K. A., & Shang, P. (Eds.). (2008). *Biracial and multiracial students* (New directions for student services, No. 123). San Francisco, CA: Jossey-Bass.

Rest, J. R. (1979). *Development in judging moral values.* Minneapolis, MN: University of Minnesota Press.

Rodriguez, A. L., Guido-DiBrito, F., Torres, V., & Talbot, D. (2000). Latina college students: Issues and challenges for the 21st Century. *Journal of Student Affairs Research and Practice, 37*(3), 511–527.

Sanford, N. (1966). *Self and society.* New York, NY: Atherton.

Schlossberg, N. K. (1981). A model for analyzing human adaptation to transition. *The Counseling Psychologist, 9*(2), 2–18. doi:10.1177/001100008100900202

Sexual Exploitation and Other Abuse of Children, 18 U.S.C. §§ 2252–2256 (2008).

Stevens, S. B., & Morris, T. L. (2007). College dating and social anxiety: Using the Internet as a means of connecting to others. *CyberPsychology and Behavior, 10*(5), 680–688.

Smolla, R. A. (2011). *The constitution goes to college: Five constitutional ideas that have shaped the American university.* New York, NY: NYU Press.

Tierney, W. G. (Ed.). (1990). Assessing academic climates and cultures (New directions for institutional research, No. 68.). San Francisco, CA: Jossey-Bass.

Tierney, W. G. (2008). *The impact of culture on organizational decision making: Theory and practice in higher education.* Sterling, VA: Stylus.

U.S. Department of Education Office for Civil Rights. (2001, January 19). *Revised sexual harassment guidance: Harassment of students by school employees, other students, or third parties.* Retrieved from http://www2.ed.gov/about/offices/list/ocr/docs/shguide.html

U.S. Department of Education Office for Civil Rights. (2011, April). *Dear colleague letter.* Retrieved from http://www2.ed.gov/about/offices/list/ocr/letters/colleague-201104.html

Weeks, D. (1992). *The eight essential steps to conflict resolution.* Los Angeles, CA: Tarcher.

Zdziarski, E. L., Dunkel, N. W., & Rollo, J. M. (2007). *Campus crisis management: A comprehensive guide to planning, prevention, response, and recovery.* San Francisco, CA: Jossey-Bass.

CHAPTER 5

Conclusion

WE BEGAN THIS book with a story about U.S. Marine Corps General James N. Mattis, who had to make a quick decision about a potential terrorist threat. When questioned about his rapid "gut" reaction, he explained that his 30-second decision was made possible by 30 years of practice and reflection. Just as the Military Decision Making Process (MDMP) provides a structure for military personnel to learn and practice decision making, our decision-making framework (DMF) offers a similar foundation for novice student affairs professionals. We hope that you are never faced with a potential terrorist attack. However, as a student affairs professional, you will likely encounter a variety of crisis situations and many relatively mundane problems that need immediate attention. Effectively solving both types of problems is imperative in student affairs work, and it requires a certain level of decision-making ability. The DMF is designed as a guide and training tool for novice student affairs professionals to use as they develop decision-making skills.

The DMF comprises a series of phases, tasks, and key considerations that can help you navigate almost any student affairs problem. In this book, we encouraged you to apply the DMF as you worked through the sample cases. We hope you will also find the DMF to be helpful in navigating real-world problems. As you continue on your professional journey, you will have a decreasing need to refer to the DMF. With practice, you will intuitively begin to identify problems, comprehensively scan your options, effectively implement solutions, and assess your decision-making processes and products. Like General Mattis and many senior student affairs professionals, you can develop a personalized and intuitive decision-making style.

Because developing an instinctual decision-making style requires practice, *Decisions Matter* includes 30 diverse case studies covering a wide range of topics, including alcohol, natural disasters, social media, group dynamics, mental health concerns, veterans affairs, and much more. The cases are intentionally situated in a variety of institutional contexts so your decision-making praxis can prepare you to work in diverse educational settings. As you applied the DMF to these case studies, you might have found yourself using the framework as designed or modifying it to fit your personal style. Either way, by learning and applying the DMF to contemporary case studies, you have begun to forge the foundation of your own personalized decision-making style.

In this book, we made the case that effective decision making is intricately related to competency development. We believe that as practitioners make decisions regarding major crises and minor events, they are simultaneously developing professional competencies. Therefore, a significant feature of *Decisions Matters* is its connection to and use of the various professional competency areas summarized in the *Professional Competency Areas for Student Affairs*

Practitioners (ACPA & NASPA, 2010). To highlight the connections between decision making and competency development, we mapped the details of the various case studies to corresponding competency areas. In the Competency Matters sections in chapter 4, we suggested ways that you might draw on particular skill sets to solve problems. Rather than being prescriptive, we tried to model a way of engaging in the decision-making process while developing proficiencies. In which professional competency areas do you feel most proficient? In which areas do you need the most development? What actions will you take to develop competencies in which you are less proficient? We hope that as you worked through the cases, you gave serious thought to these questions and to methods for increasing your professional competencies.

FINAL REFLECTIONS

One of the kernels of knowledge that we want you take away from this book is the significance of reflection and assessment in decision making. Phase 4 of the DMF provides structure for assessment by asking questions that invite you to reflect on both the outcomes and processes of your decision making. In the fast-paced world of student affairs work, thoughtful reflection can seem like a luxury; however, growing and developing as a decision maker requires candid reflection on the impact of your decisions and the process by which you made them. We hope that as you develop and hone your own intuitive decision-making style, thoughtful deliberation becomes second nature. In an effort to model reflection, the four authors decided to end this book by reflecting on the process of crafting the DMF and writing *Decisions Matter*.

Annemarie

One of the foundations of student affairs work is to promote the holistic development of students. Holistic practice is most effective when student affairs professionals collaborate with each other *and* with academic partners. As a faculty member, I teach graduate students about the necessity of developing working relationships with staff and faculty across campus. Collaborating with Delight, Brian, and Mike to write *Decisions Matters* reaffirmed for me how important such partnerships can be. I believe that *Decisions Matter* is a more comprehensive and insightful book because of our collaborative partnership.

In this concluding chapter, I would like to reiterate that there is no single or correct way to respond to contemporary student affairs problems. The four authors come from unique life trajectories, theoretical perspectives, and bases of expertise. Thus, our answers to the DMF questions were often slightly different. Our process of writing this book and working through the sample case was one of listening, learning, and continuous reflection. As with any collaboration, we had moments of disagreement and times of inspired creativity. Through our collective decision-making process, I learned much from my colleagues. Brian is a vice president for student affairs whose daily work focuses on legal issues, policy, and precedent. Delight, on the other hand, is a faculty member who hails from a counseling background. Her contribution was to ensure that interpersonal issues, helping skills, and advising best practices were considered. Mike's emphasis on organizational theory and the salience of context pervaded all of our conversations about the DMF. I am a critical scholar who sees higher education through a particular set of lenses. Issues of justice, power, inequality, and social identity are at the forefront of how I approach life in general and the DMF questions in particular. As I responded to the sample case, "To Tweet or Not to Tweet," my gut instinct was first and foremost to consider issues of safety. However, my second instinctual emphasis in the sample case was to analyze and respond to issues of justice and inequality. At the same time, my co-authors brought their unique instinctual emphases (e.g., law, counseling, organizational theory) to the table. As we wrestled with the sample case and debated our responses, I was reminded of the importance of collaborative learning.

Typically, when we think of partnerships in student affairs, we envision structured programs and planned campus initiatives. My experience working through the sample case with Brian, Delight, and Mike reminded me that collaborating on everyday decision making is equally as important. Just as *Decisions Matter* is a better book as a result of our collaboration, our responses to the sample case were also more comprehensive. Each of us contributed his or her instinctual reactions and professional expertise. The combination of diverse perspectives allowed us to more thoroughly analyze the case study and brainstorm a wider array of possible solutions. While each of us could have independently managed a situation similar to the sample case, our collective perspective was richer than any one of our individual responses would have been. As you worked through the case studies in this book, did you consider how your perspectives were different from or similar to those of your classmates or colleagues? Or were you tempted to dismiss different opinions? I hope you welcomed and learned from the perspectives of your peers and colleagues—such openness to collaborative learning will help you be more effective as a practitioner. Remember, effective decision makers reflect on both the process *and* product of their decisions. What better way to do this than by learning from others?

Mike

In reflecting on the importance of this book and lessons learned along the way, it occurred to me that working with case studies is a bit like working with clay. The creative process combines with the malleable nature of the product and gives sculptors (in this case, Delight, Annemarie, Brian, and me) the opportunity to set a scene, populate it with academic characters, and add shades of local color, nuanced details, and other textures. To extend the metaphor, it is a luxury to be able to demolish a scenario that is not working and start again. Anyone who has ever dismantled a work in progress and collected the raw clay materials back into a heaping ball might have experienced such a cathartic moment.

In dealing with the problems, issues, and challenges we face in our daily work, however, we do not have the luxury of deconstructing and reconstructing scenarios in ways that are clean and logical. Too often, we run into situations in which a crisis has occurred and the clay is dried—that is, the damage has been done—and we must set about the task of working the problem, assessing the damage, managing collateral damage, and finding rational solutions. We are left with a product that was shaped by hands other than our own and we must try to remedy the situation.

Drawing from our collective professional experiences and long work in the field as professors and practitioners, I think we have produced a book that respects the power of working through problem situations in simulated environments and honors the real-life problems that educators face every day. The DMF that Delight, Annemarie, Brian, and I created was designed as a tool to help solve problems in both arenas.

The book stemmed primarily from conversations about the need for case study literature in the profession that is at once scholarly and practical. Above all, this undertaking represented the convergence of four close colleagues who share mutually reinforcing ideas about the importance of effective decision making for new professionals in our field. In bringing ourselves to the task, we brought our stories as well. I learned to navigate the higher education landscape working in a series of positions at a small private liberal arts college in north Georgia; each day as a new professional felt like a micro case study within the context of a larger institutional case. Through my work there and in other positions since then, I have found that the higher education landscape leaves no shortage of material for case study work—no matter how outrageous a manufactured case study might seem, we can always find a real-life situation that goes a step beyond.

The authors had many spirited discussions about the case studies and the importance of working through problems and using the DMF as both a tool and a guide. The phrase that came to mind again and again in our group work sessions was "Context is everything." As a student and scholar of the role of campus culture in shaping our views, beliefs, and behavioral norms, I have long considered the notion of context to be preeminent. Each college or university, and every department and office within that institution, has unique cultural components that influence ideas and behaviors alike. Thus, each event, crisis, problem, challenge, and solution has a unique set of cultural properties within a particular context. It is tempting to apply previously constructed templates to newly developing problems, but if we do not work within the context of each problem we risk failing in our attempt to find plausible solutions. So, details matter, and context matters more.

Delight

Simple decisions can profoundly affect our lives. When I was approached by Brian, Annemarie, and Mike to co-author a case study book, I took a few days to respond. It seemed simple enough: an introduction, a few cases, and a concluding chapter. I asked myself if I had time to work on such a project and if this project was worthy of my time. I thought about possible conflicts, such as meeting times and the number of hours writing such a book might take. The project seemed interesting and I was acquainted with the members of the group, who were likeable, so I said yes.

What I did not consider was the journey we were about to undertake. Decisions lead us on paths that are often unpredictable and have outcomes that we cannot anticipate. At the start of the book project, we were immersed in deciding how we would collect real-life cases, giving a lot of thought to how we might solicit cases from our colleagues. We brainstormed vehicles for obtaining and storing cases. Because three of us came from the academic side of the house, we also wanted our book to be based solidly on research, so we began looking at decision-making theories and models that might guide readers as they reasoned out their own decisions for the various cases. As it turned out, none of the models seemed to fit the needs of emerging student affairs professionals, and none took the new professional competencies (ACPA & NASPA, 2010) into account. So it was a natural shift into developing our own DMF and structuring the book to include the competencies in the discussion. I discovered that simple decisions—such as deciding to work on a case study book—are never really simple.

The beauty of this increasingly complex project was its power to make us better thinkers and force us to spend more time together. We had endless hours of meetings and discussions. Many aspects of our personal lives wove their way into our meetings; so, too, did a lot of humor. As we struggled with our own group decisions, we developed friendships that might never otherwise have happened. Ultimately, my simple decision to join my three co-authors yielded a book I am proud of and relationships that will last a lifetime. Whenever a person or a group makes a decision, however simple or complex, changes occur in their life. Decisions lead us on paths that are often unpredictable and have outcomes that we really cannot anticipate.

Brian

When I think back to my early days as a new professional, making decisions (typically on the fly) was the most intimidating aspect of my work. What if I made the wrong decision? Would I be fired? What if I put someone's safety at risk? Even in the smallest matters, I was always nervous about the outcomes of my actions. But I have learned that as you progress in your career, you will develop a pattern or particular approach to problem solving. In many ways, it will become rote. Or— as in the case of General Mattis described in the introduction to this book—decision making will become intuitive and instinctual.

In creating the DMF, Annemarie, Delight, Mike, and I thought about a logical sequence of reflection and action, suggesting that pausing to think before you act gives you the ability to judge a variety of variables associated with decision making. *Decisions Matter* offers you the chance to develop your own pattern of decision making in a step-by-step fashion, with full knowledge that sometimes events do not occur in a linear fashion. Using the DMF as a training tool and applying it to the cases in this book gives you the opportunity to hone your decision-making skills in a safe, nonjudgmental manner. The cases are simulations, so your decisions cannot hurt anyone. Take risks with the cases, change the context of the situations, and consider other variables. In addition, consistently revisit the basic, intermediate, and advanced professional competencies in conjunction with *Decisions Matter*. Which competencies are you most comfortable with? Which ones do you still need to learn and master? Continue to practice and eventually you will find that you have the tools to develop a style of decision making that works best for you.

If you are wondering whether the nervousness about making the right decision ever goes away, I have to admit that, despite my years of experience and the number of large and small situations I have had to manage, the nervousness never goes away. But I realize that with each new challenge, I have become more confident in my decisions. Sometimes my gut reaction is a result of trial-and-error or a simple hope and prayer. Most often, however, as a vice president for student affairs, my intuitive decision-making style is a product of more than 25 years of experience and practice. I hope that as you work through the cases in this book and practice applying the DMF, you will gain confidence in both the outcomes and process of your simulated *and* real-life decisions. If so, you are on your way to developing an intuitive decision-making style that you can call your own.

List of Cases by Category

History, Philosophy, and Values

Human and Organizational Resources

Law, Policy, and Governance

Leadership

Personal Foundations

Student Learning and Development

INSTITUTIONAL CHARACTERISTICS

Public

Private

DEPARTMENTS/FUNCTIONAL AREAS

New Student Programs

Nontraditional Student Services

Residence Life

Service-Learning/Civic Engagement

Student Activities

Student Conduct

Women's Center

TOPIC AREAS

Gay, Lesbian, Bisexual, Transgender Issues

Group Dynamics

Immigration

Learning Differences

Legal Issues (Local, State, Federal)

Mental Health Issues

Multicultural Issues

Natural Disaster

Nontraditional Students

Professional Ethics

Religion

Roommate Conflicts

Supervision

Index